Brian Friel

Twayne's English Authors Series

Kinley E. Roby

Northeastern University

TEAS 470

BRIAN FRIEL
(1929-)
Portrait by Basil Blackshaw

Brian Friel

By George O'Brien

Georgetown University

Twayne Publishers
A Division of G. K. Hall & Co. • *Boston*

Brian Friel
George O'Brien

Copyright 1990 by G. K. Hall & Co.
All rights reserved.
Published by Twayne Publishers
A Division of G. K. Hall & Co.
70 Lincoln Street
Boston, Massachusetts 02111

Copyediting supervised by Barbara Sutton
Book production by Patricia D'Agostino
Book design by Barbara Anderson

Typeset in 11 pt. Garamond
by Compositors Corporation

Printed on permanent/durable acid-free paper
and bound in the United States of America

Library of Congress Cataloging-in-Publication Data

O'Brien, George, 1945–
    Brian Friel / by George O'Brien.
        p.   cm. — (Twayne's English authors series ; TEAS 470)
    Bibliography: p.
    Includes index.
    ISBN 0-8057-6980-3 (alk. paper)
    1. Friel, Brian—Criticism and interpretation.   I. Title.
II. Series.
PR6056.R5Z84   1989
822'.914—dc20   89-15215
                                                          CIP

Contents

About the Author

George O'Brien was born in Ireland in 1945 and educated there, at Ruskin College, Oxford, and at the University of Warwick, where he received his B.A. and Ph.D. He held teaching positions at Warwick and at Clare College, Cambridge, and after moving to the United States was a visiting assistant professor of English at Vassar College from 1980 to 1984, since which time he has held a similar position at Georgetown University. He has published articles on Irish literature in England, Ireland and the United States.

O'Brien received a Hennessy/New Irish Writing award for his short fiction in 1973 and won an *Ulster Tatler* short story prize in 1977. His memoir, *The Village of Longing: An Irish Boyhood in the Fifties* (Lilliput Press, 1987), was nominated by the noted Irish poet Seamus Heaney as one of his "Books of the Year" for 1987 in the London *Observer*. A sequel, *Dancehall Days*, was published in 1988. Both titles will be published in England by Penguin Books in 1989.

Professor O'Brien lives in northern Virginia with his wife and two sons.

Preface

It has become a commonplace of recent Irish theatrical history to make such statements as, "Brian Friel . . . has consistently proved himself to be Ireland's most substantial dramatist—Samuel Beckett apart—over two decades."[1] Early in his career he was named as one of a quartet of playwriting contemporaries who "can easily hold their own with any quartet of current playwrights one could mention from England, France, or America."[2] Friel's plays have been credited with being "the body of work most distinguished by its substance, integrity, and development"[3] of all the drama produced by his generation of Irish playwrights. His achievement is all the more significant in an Irish context since "he is a Northern Catholic, the first important dramatist from that background"[4]—and certainly the first dramatist from that background to make a substantial contribution to Irish cultural politics, by his plays, by the establishment in 1980 of the Field Day Theatre Company, and, since 1983, by the publication of the Field Day pamphlet series.

Yet to some extent (and partly because of his background) Friel is an unlikely literary luminary. In his own words: "There was no background of writing in my family and I don't know how much of my talent is indigenous."[5] Moreover, he lacks the public notoriety frequently courted by Irish literary figures, particularly those connected with the theater. In contrast to such stage Irishmen, Friel has been described as "the opposite of cityish, witty, urbane, forceful."[6] His public demeanor and sense of his status seem directly related to his experience of the writing life as "a very private and personal existence."[7] Yet, like the outsiders who are the most influential figures in his plays and stories, the apparent remoteness of privacy has paradoxically ensured his "exemplary"[8] position in Irish drama at a testing period in its development.[9] And, though he would understandably resist the label, he has become an elder statesman of Ulster writing. This is not to suggest that his significance is limited to the cultural concerns of his native province. Still, Friel's career is exemplary in its fidelity to his origins, its implicit belief that he could speak in his work to, and on behalf of, his immediate public. Friel has also revealed a strong strain of independence in his commitment to artistic development and to the creation of a theatrical idiom that, because of its novel and idiosyncratic use of the form, bears the impress of a mind thinking for itself.

Thus, Friel's career is culturally and historically significant because of its origins and background and because of his response to its formative conditions. This response is notable for its persistence, its variety, and the uncompromised humanity of its vision, in which the image of the human is dignified by Friel's patient, tolerant, generous disposition. The relevance of such values for Irish audiences, north and south of the Border, at a time when their societies are undergoing painful reappraisal, is self-evident. As Friel's numerous international successes indicate, however, the appeal of his thought and art is not confined to one particular audience. In ways that the reception of his work in Ireland has not always acknowledged or accepted, Friel has contributed to the inversion of one of the traditional mainstays of Irish writing by drawing attention to the general human dimension of Irish experience rather than to the specifically Irish character of human experience. For this reason, too, Friel's work has a significance that, though based on its theatrical attainments, ultimately exceeds them, making his name inseparable from the travails of Irish culture as, fifty years after its institutional ratification in the Irish Free State and the Stormont governments, it seeks to redefine itself.

This book is an introduction to and critical commentary on the work of Brian Friel. The approach throughout is critical and cultural, rather than, for example, sociological or historical. In chapter 1, after providing a brief biography of Friel, I assess his work as a storywriter and establish its relationship to his more substantial career as a playwright. In chapter 2 I deal with Friel's early, unpublished work for radio and for the stage and conclude with a discussion of his early dramatic successes, one of which, *Philadelphia, Here I Come!*, remains his most popular play.

Chapter 3 goes on to characterize Friel's development as a playwright during the 1960s, with particular emphasis on his dramaturgical innovations. His strong reliance on one central character in the 1960s plays is also analyzed under the heading "Friel's Theater of Character." The chapter concludes with an account of Friel's early attempts to make a transition to a more obviously culturally concerned and communally oriented theater.

Chapter 4 covers Friel's plays from the early 1970s (*The Freedom of the City*, 1973) to the late 1980s (*Making History*, 1988). Again the emphasis is on Friel's thematic and structural developments, which are identified in his establishment of a "Theatre of Fact," in his more intense and more sophisticated reestablishment of the family as one of his central dramatic concerns, and finally in the creation of "Friel's Theater of Language." The concluding chapter 5 is a brief overview of Friel's achievement in the theater and the significance of his work in contemporary Irish literary culture.

I wish to express my gratitude to the following for favors received.

Extracts from the plays *Philadelphia, Here I Come!*, *The Lovers of Cass McGuire, Crystal and Fox, Lovers, The Freedom of the City, Volunteers, Living Quarters, Faith Healer, Translations, The Communication Cord,* and *Fathers and Sons* are reprinted by permission of Faber and Faber Limited.

Extracts from *The Saucer of Larks* and *The Gold in the Sea* are reproduced by permission of Curtis Brown Ltd., London. © Brian Friel.

Extracts from *The Gentle Island* are reprinted by permission of Reg Davis-Poynter.

Extracts from *The Enemy Within, Aristocrats, Three Sisters,* and *Selected Stories* are reprinted by permission of the Gallery Press.

Extracts from *Brian Friel* by D. E. S. Maxwell are reprinted by permission of Associated University Presses.

Extracts from *Brian Friel: The Growth of an Irish Dramatist* by Ulf Dantanus are reprinted by kind permission of the author.

In addition, to Mr. Friel, for permission to quote from his works, for the generosity and promptness of his response to my inquiries, and for other kindnesses.

To Basil Blackshaw, for his portrait of Brian Friel used as the frontispiece.

To Professor James F. Slevin, Chairman of the Department of English, Georgetown University, and Father Royden B. Davis, S.J., Dean of the College of Arts and Sciences, Georgetown University, for a summer free of teaching.

To Dr. Marie-Helen Gibney and Father J. Donald Freeze, Provost, Georgetown University, for assistance from the Provost's Publication Fund.

To Mr. Gary McKeone, for providing indispensable photocopies, interest, and enthusiasm.

To Mr. John Evans, for his research efforts and for his friendship.

To Mr. Christopher Griffin, for access to his enviable and invaluable Irish Theatre archive.

To Professor Anthony Bradley, for sharing his thoughts on Friel and for the best of good talk.

To Mrs. Joan Reuss, for prodigious feats of word-processing and patience.

And not least, to my family—Pam, Ben, and Nick—for somehow managing to remain their usual vital, loving selves during the interminable season of "Daddy is working." To them I dedicate my work, with love.

Needless to say, none of the above is responsible for any errors of fact, phrasing, tact, or judgment this book may contain. That responsibility is mine alone.

George O'Brien

Georgetown University

Chronology

1929   Brian Friel born 9 January in Omagh, County Tyrone, Northern Ireland.

1939   Family moves to city of Derry, Northern Ireland.

1939–1945   Education: Long Tower School and Saint Columb's College, Derry.

1945–1948   Education: Maynooth College, County Kildare, Eire (the National Seminary); graduates with B.A.

1949–1950   Education: Saint Joseph's Teacher Training College, Belfast, Northern Ireland.

1950–1960   Teaches in Derry; begins writing short stories; regular appearances in the *New Yorker* begin with "The Skelper," August, 1959.

1954   Marries Anne Morrison.

1958   First play, *A Sort of Freedom*, written for radio, broadcast on BBC Northern Ireland Home Service.

1959   First stage play, *The Francophile (A Doubtful Paradise)*, performed at Group Theatre, Belfast.

1960   Retires from teaching.

1962   English and American editions of first book of stories, *A Saucer of Larks*. *The Enemy Within* premieres, Abbey Theatre, Dublin.

1963   *The Blind Mice* premieres, Eblana Theatre, Dublin. April-May, student of dramaturgy at the Guthrie Theater, Minneapolis.

1964   First major play, *Philadelphia, Here I Come!*, is the hit of that year's Dublin Theatre Festival.

1966   First international production, *Philadelphia, Here I Come!*, on Broadway. English and American publication of second book of stories, *The Gold in the Sea*. Second international production, premiere on Broadway of *The Loves of Cass McGuire*.

1967   *Lovers: Winners and Losers* premieres, Gate Theatre, Dublin.

1968   *Crystal and Fox* premieres, Gaiety Theatre, Dublin.

1969   *The Mundy Scheme* premieres, Olympia Theatre, Dublin.

1970   *The Gentle Island* premieres, Olympia Theatre, Dublin.

1972   Elected member of the Irish Academy of Letters.

1973   *The Freedom of the City* premieres, Abbey Theatre, Dublin.

1975   *Volunteers* premieres, Abbey Theatre, Dublin.

1977   *Living Quarters* premieres, Abbey Theatre, Dublin.

1979   *Aristocrats* premieres, Abbey Theatre, Dublin. *Faith Healer* premieres, Longacre Theatre, New York.

1980   Foundation of Field Day Theatre Company. *Translations*, Field Day's first production, premieres, Guildhall, Derry.

1981   *Translations* awarded the Ewart-Biggs Peace Prize. Friel's translation of Chekhov's *Three Sisters* premieres, Guildhall, Derry.

1982   *The Communication Cord* premieres, Guildhall, Derry. Elected member of Aosdana, the national treasury of Irish artists.

1983   Awarded honorary D. Litt. by National University of Ireland.

1987   Accepts nomination to the Irish Senate. Adaptation of Turgenev's *Fathers and Sons* premieres, National Theatre, London.

1988   *Making History* premieres, Guildhall, Derry.

Chapter One

Storyteller and Playwright

Brian Friel was born near Omagh, County Tyrone, Northern Ireland on 9 January 1929. His father, a native of Derry, taught at a local primary school. Friel's mother was from Donegal, where the author-to-be frequently spent holidays that were to have a formative effect on his imagination, as his stories in particular suggest, and that no doubt influenced his view of himself as "a sort of peasant at heart."[1] He has lived in rural County Donegal since 1969, and the generic village of Ballybeg where many of his plays are set is (to cite a typical reference) located "in a remote part of County Donegal"[2]—than which it is difficult to imagine a place more remote.

The appeal of the rural hinterland of Donegal was enhanced by the relocation of the family in Derry city when Friel was ten, his father having transferred to a teaching position in the Long Tower school there. Friel attended this school before completing his secondary education at Saint Columb's College, Derry. From there he went to Saint Patrick's College, Maynooth, the Republic of Ireland's national seminary near Dublin. Friel spent two-and-a-half years here, and has referred to it as "a very disturbing experience."[3] Instead of going on for the priesthood, as might be expected of a seminarist, he graduated with a B.A. and took a postgraduate teacher-training course at Saint Joseph's College, Belfast. By 1950 Friel's formal education was complete. For the next ten years, following in the professional footsteps of his father and two sisters, he taught school in Derry.

Since terms such as *Northern Ireland*, *Ulster*, and *Border* will recur throughout much of what follows, it seems appropriate at this point to provide a brief sketch of the larger sociopolitical background in which Friel grew up. The Irish province of Ulster consists of the island's nine northernmost counties. When juridical and administrative autonomy within the British Empire seemed imminent in the early years of the twentieth century, as a result of constitutional agitation for Home Rule for Ireland, the predominantly Protestant population of Ulster's northeastern counties resisted the possibility. The fruit of their loyalty to the British crown, and the reward for their political party, the Unionists, was the establishment of a parliament to rule the six loyal counties. Provisions for this state to come into being were made in the Government of Ireland Act, 1920, and the Northern parliament was opened in 1921, shortly before the signing of the treaty bringing to an end hostilities between Crown forces and the twenty-six nationalist, predominantly Catholic counties that made up the rest of Ireland. Thus Ireland was partitioned, and the Border between the island's two jurisdictions has remained a painful source of contention.

In addition, the defensiveness from which the Northern Ireland state originally arose became enshrined in its social policies and public institutions: "the course of events subsequently tended to perpetuate divisions and perpetuate allegiances."[4] Derry, Northern Ireland's second largest city, had since the state's inception suffered in a particularly blatant fashion from the ruling Unionist party's juridical and social inequities. Despite the majority of its citizens being Catholic Nationalists, they had virtually no chance of replacing the monopoly of Protestant Unionists on the city council, a monopoly maintained by careful gerrymandering of the city's electoral wards and by plural voting rights based on property holding. Friel's father was active in Nationalist circles in the town, as was Friel himself for a period. But the combination of social deprivation and political frustration had a strongly alienating effect, as Friel later recalled: "The sense of frustration which I felt under the tight and immovable Unionist regime became distasteful."[5]

There is no evidence to suggest that Friel's career as a writer began as an expression of withdrawal from, and implicit resistance to, the atmosphere of Derry in the 1950s. As the subsequent discussion of his early stories will point out, the stories delineate stagnation and limitation and the occasional moment of bittersweet illumination. What is notable in the formative years of Friel's career is his commitment to writing, which cannot have been easy while carrying on a full-time teaching career and becoming a family man (he married Anne Morrison in 1954, and they have four daughters and a son). Clearly he was helped by a contract with the *New Yorker*, which had first refusal on his stories. By 1960, the year that Friel quit teaching to write full-time, he had published many of the short stories collected in *The Saucer of Larks* (1962), and he had had his first dramatic efforts—for radio—accepted. At this point, Friel was preeminently a short story writer, working in the essentially pastoral mode of the Irish short story in the interwar period, whose best-known exponents are Frank O'Connor and Sean O'Faolain, though Friel's work is nearer in tone and touch to the lesser known and unjustly neglected Ulster story writer, Michael McLaverty.

Two radio plays, *A Sort of Freedom* and *To This Hard House*, were broadcast in 1958. Both are not quite conclusive evidence in support of Friel's admission that, "As for playwriting it began as a sort of self-indulgence and then eventually I got caught up more and more in it."[6] Compared to the deftness of his stories, however, they are stiff and overearnest. Yet within five years Friel's theatrical entanglement had become so severe that to take charge of it he spent three months in early 1963 at the Guthrie Theater in Minneapolis, Minnesota, to observe Sir Tyrone Guthrie rehearse *Hamlet* and Chekhov's *Three Sisters* for that theater's inaugural season. This sojourn and the risky decision three years earlier to resign from teaching mark the decisive turning points in Friel's career.

The Guthrie Theater commemorates by name the rich theatrical legacy of its founder, Sir Tyrone Guthrie. A veteran of theater in England of the 1930s and 1940s, when he was closely associated with London's famous Old Vic Theatre and had directed all the luminaries of the English stage— Charles Laughton, Laurence Olivier, Flora Robson, John Gielgud, Ralph Richardson—Guthrie had an equally illustrious set of international credentials. One of his most enduring achievements is the foundation of the Stratford, Ontario, Shakespeare Festival, a landmark on the North American theater calendar since Guthrie began it in 1952. Guthrie also revolutionized postwar theater design with his innovative use of the thrust stage—a stage that breaks the conventional boundary of the proscenium arch by thrusting itself into the body of the audience, which as a result is more directly affected by and intimately associated with the drama. In all, Guthrie was a consummate man of the theater and ambitious in his sense of the theater's importance, as the confession of faith made at the close of his autobiography, *A Life in the Theatre*, makes clear: "I believe that the purpose of the theatre is to show mankind to himself, and thereby to show to man God's image."[7] These qualifications, together with the fact that Guthrie had Ulster connections (though he was born in England, his family home, to which he retired and where he died, was in County Monaghan), ensured that the four months Friel spent in Minneapolis were crucially instructive, particularly in view of his belief that "indigenous drama was a valuable element in both national development and international understanding; that art *must* spring from the soil; that to be authentic was important in speech and action, not just on the stage but always and everywhere."[8]

The immediate result of Friel's journey to Minneapolis was his first and largest hit, *Philadelphia, Here I Come!*, which, apart from its innovative use of two actors to play two different aspects of the protagonist, enabled Friel to present a more vivid and complex set of perspectives on familiar material: "It was a play about an area of Irish life that I had been closely associated with in County Donegal. Our neighbours and friends there had all been affected by emigration . . ."[9] (though Friel goes on to say that the play's subject is love

rather than emigration). Friel's post-Minneapolis attitude toward his material is informed by the same affections and attachments as previously, but
disciplined now by a much more sophisticated sense of theatrical possibility
and aesthetic distancing. The plays immediately following *Philadelphia*
(those produced between 1964 and 1968) certainly bear witness to Friel's
rapidly developing dramaturgical mastery.

In 1969 Friel offered a new play, *The Mundy Scheme*, to the Abbey Theatre, Dublin—Ireland's national theater—which rejected it. The play marks,
in Friel's words, "a completely new direction"[10] in his work, and has for its
subject the farcical, self-serving, self-aggrandizing character of contemporary
Irish politics. At the same time, however, political activity in Northern Ireland was taking a decisively violent turn. Demonstrations and protest
marches in support of civil rights for the minority population incurred a
wrathful, violent reaction at the grassroots level of Unionism. This reaction
led to the introduction of British troops to keep the peace between the two
communities. In response to this move, violent elements on the minority side
took arms against the troops.

The enumeration of atrocities and aborted political initiatives resulting
from the violent polarization of Catholic Nationalist and Protestant Unionist
factions is beside the point of the present purpose. It must be noted, however,
that in the case of Derry, the climactic episode of civil disorder was the killing
of thirteen civil rights protesters by British troops during a demonstration on
30 January 1972, subsequently known as Bloody Sunday. Prior to this event,
Friel had said that because "I have no objectivity in this situation" and "I
don't think there is the stuff of drama in the situation"[11] he could not envisage writing a play about it. This attitude changed substantially: *The Freedom
of the City*, first produced in 1973, is based on the events of Bloody Sunday
and its aftermath and introduces a more public, communal, cultural, and
historical set of themes to Friel's work. The increasing intellectual complexity
and dramaturgical finesse with which Friel treats these themes in his plays of
the 1970s find their most elaborate expression in his most admired play,
Translations, which had its first night in the Guildhall, Derry, a building that
is a symbol of power and alienation in *The Freedom of the City*.

Translations was the first production of the Field Day Theatre Company,
founded in 1980 by Friel and the actor Stephen Rea. The company has produced most of Friel's plays since *Translations*, has commissioned work from
some of the finest contemporary Irish writers,[12] and has toured Ireland, north
and south, with its productions, "adding to the artistic links which are being
forged."[13] In 1983 a directorate of Field Day was formed, consisting of such
prominent Northern Ireland poets and intellectuals as Seamus Heaney,

Seamus Deane, and Tom Paulin. (Friel, Rea, and the noted Northern Ireland broadcaster David Hammond complete the directorate.) The immediate result of this development was publication of the first three of a series of controversial pamphlets.

It is unlikely that Friel believed that Field Day's purpose should be the same as the one he suggested to the editors of a local Derry magazine in 1970: "The editors of a little magazine must have one purpose and a total conviction of their ability to achieve it: their purpose must be to change the face of the earth."[14] Nevertheless, there is no doubting the commitment of Field Day in its pamphlet form:

In brief, all the directors felt that the political crisis in the North and its reverberations in the Republic had made the necessity of a reappraisal of Ireland's political and cultural situation explicit and urgent. All the directors are northerners. They believed that Field Day could and should contribute to the solution of the present crisis by producing analyses of the established opinions, myths and stereotypes which had become both a symptom and a cause of the current situation. The collapse of constitutional and political arrangements and the recrudescence of the violence which they had been designed to repress or contain, made this a more urgent requirement in the North than in the Republic, even though the improbability of either surviving in its present form seemed clear in 1980 and is clearer still in 1985.[15]

Initially concerned with literary and cultural topics, the pamphlet series has subsequently broadened its scope to deal with historical and juridical areas. The effect of these pamphlets has been considerable, and they have fueled the contemporary debate about past and future in Irish thought.[16]

Friel has received many of the honors that his country gives to writers. He was elected to the Irish Academy of Letters in 1972 and became a member of Aosdana, the national treasury of Irish artists, in 1982. The National University of Ireland granted him an honorary D.Litt. in 1982. In honor of his cultural commitment, and also, no doubt, his artistic achievements, Brian Friel was nominated in 1986 to a seat in the Irish Senate, the consultative lower house of the Irish Parliament. He accepted this unusual nomination and is the first Irish writer to serve in this capacity since the poet W. B. Yeats, whose term as senator came to an end in 1928, the year before Friel was born.

The World of the Stories

Between the appearance of his first short story, "The Child"[17] and the publication of *The Gold in the Sea*, Brian Friel had an extremely successful career as a writer of stories. Two collections—a total of thirty-one stories in all[18]—

were published and received a generous critical reception from such notables as Sir Tyrone Guthrie and Edna O'Brien; and their judgment has been endorsed by the eminent English critic Walter Allen, who considers Friel "a natural story-writer" who "accepts his findings about life . . . without reservations and . . . transmits admirably the feel of ordinary life."[19] These books were reviewed in prestigious newspapers and periodicals, and both had British and American editions. Such attention was merely a ratification of the already high profile acquired by the stories as a result of their initial publication in such periodicals as the *New Yorker* and the *Atlantic Monthly*. In short, from the beginning Friel's work has won and held an international audience.

As *The Saucer of Larks: Stories of Ireland* (a selection of stories from *The Saucer of Larks* and *The Gold in the Sea*) makes clear, there is little sense of development in Friel's story-writing. He came to his world and its themes early and, rather uncritically, remained with them until committing himself completely to the theater. This is not to say that all of Friel's stories are alike, or that their world gains in blandness what it fails to attain in diversity. On the contrary, they contain a variety of themes and a reasonably broad spectrum of character. It is fair to say, however, that each bears a family resemblance to the others. Beneath their circumstantial differences and somewhat differentiated personnel, Friel's stories possess an essential kinship. And while on the one hand the stories' family likeness tends to blur their particularities, it also alerts the reader to the possibility that the combination of likenesses ultimately make up an articulate map of an integrated imaginative world.

Friel's primary source for this world, and a fundamental ground for its imaginative integration, is the landscape of his childhood. In D. E. S. Maxwell's words: "The 'real' world of Brian Friel's short stories reaches from Kincasslagh in the west of Donegal through Strabane, Derry City, and Coleraine to Omagh and County Tyrone."[20] In fact, as Maxwell points out, Derry City, Friel's home town, does not feature very prominently in the stories; only Johnny and Mick" (*SOL*, 133–43) seems to be set in it (while Derry is undeniably the story's setting, the city remains unnamed).[21] Thus, the stories' terrain is that of the author's preadolescent years. Broadly speaking, the landscape is that of the Northwest quadrant of Ulster, in particular the northwest corner of County Tyrone and the county to the immediate northwest of that, Donegal.

To most of Friel's readers, including many in Ireland, this stretch of country is virtually a definition of remoteness and unfamiliarity. Most Irish readers, however, would note that Friel treats it in a revealingly anachronistic manner by ignoring the Border, which divides it. County Tyrone falls under the jurisdiction of the British Government, and from 1920 to 1973 was within the remit of a parliament in Belfast. County Donegal, on the other hand, is in Eire, the Irish Republic. Friel in his stories remains as oblivious of the Border as the youthful narrator of "Mr. Sing My Heart's Delight," traveling "the forty-five-mile journey by train, mail car, and foot across County Donegal to my granny's house which sat at the top of a cliff above the raging Atlantic at the very end of the parish of Mullaghduff" (*SOL*, 168).

Friel's apparent indifference to the Border has elicited a certain amount of critical comment: "In his Irish context there is no place for the Border, and it does not seem to exist in his writing, where his characters, especially in the short stories and early plays, move from west to east and from north to south without the Border being mentioned. . . . Friel frequently deals, both directly and indirectly, with the tragic consequences of Partition, but his subject matter is the whole island of Ireland."[22] This statement enlarges Sean MacMahon's comment, particularly apropos Friel's stories, that the Border "seems not yet to have affected his writing"[23] The alternative approach, of course, is that of John Wilson Foster in his *Forces and Themes in Ulster Fiction*: "It seemed best . . . to disregard the border as a precise cultural divide."[24]

Friel's exclusion from his fictional world of this basic fact of sociopolitical life may be interpreted in a variety of ways. There is a dearth of evidence for the assertion that the Border is sublimated by the author's all-Irish concerns. As to Sean MacMahon's point, it all depends on what *affect* means, as we shall see. Moreover, it is not true that Friel completely overlooks the Border issues. The stories "Johnny and Mick" and "The Death of a Scientific Humanist" (*GIS*, 55–68) examine aspects of a Border-influenced reality. The former story has at its core a sense of irreparable, unconscious social division, while the latter can be read as an oblique, vaguely satirical commentary on Ulster's religious narrow-mindedness. If, in general, Friel's stories studiously avoid the Border, they remain even more silent about the fact that their domain is almost identical to that of the ancient tribal lands of the powerful O'Neill and O'Donnell clans, the last of the native Irish polity to resist the Elizabethan colonization of Ireland. It is undoubtedly true that "the territory of Brian Friel's short stories and plays is that borderland of Derry, Donegal, and Tyrone in which a large Catholic community leads a reduced existence under the pressure of political and economic oppression."[25]

Ultimately, however, Friel speaks for a culture, not a polity. At the same time, there is a strong sense of division in the world of Friel's stories. Indeed, the existence of two worlds is evident in the actual landscape itself. Of Tyrone it has been said that, "though a large and pleasing area, [it] is lacking somewhat in special interests, topographical, biological, or archaeological . . . a

8 BRIAN FRIEL

curiously negative tract, with a paucity of outstanding features."²⁶ The same
author writes of Donegal, however: "there is nowhere else where the beauties
of hill and dale, lake and rock, sea and bog, pasture and tillage, are so intimately and closely interwoven, so that every turn of the road opens new prospects, and every hill-crest fresh combinations of these delightful elements."²⁷
Friel doesn't necessarily endorse these views: Mullaghduff, in "Mr. Sing My
Heart's Delight," for example, is "even on the best day in summer . . . a
desolate place" (SOL, 169). For Friel, however, the issue is not topographical:
the prominent foregrounding of character in his stories is much more to the
point.

The divisions are between different areas of life. One area is the world of
work, duty, and the discipline of family structure, and has the general label
Tyrone. The other is a world of play and the relaxation of family constraints—an asocial world. This is generally known as Donegal. Thus while
both worlds contain poverty, the repressive social character of poverty is examined in a story set in a field in County Tyrone ("The Potato Gatherers,"
SOL, 79–89), while in "Mr. Sing My Heart's Delight" Granny almost in the
same breath exclaims "We are poor people here! We have nothing!" and "A
feast it'll be then. . . . A feast and be damned to Sunday" (SOL, 176), expressing a purely personal overriding of poverty.

In "A Man's World" (SOL, 106–15), the difference between the workaday
Tyrone world and the Donegal world of holiday is made explicit. Here, however, the narrator learns that such demarcations are not permanent; neither
world protects its people from their weaknesses. It may be argued that in
Friel's Donegal stories, "poverty is presented as a condition of life, a natural
and unavoidable part of the community,"²⁸ but clearly the poverty endured
by Granny in "Mr. Sing My Heart's Delight" is less corrosive than that which
seems the unhappy birthright of the child laborers in "The Potato Gatherers."
In the latter case, the impersonally mechanical source of their work (the
farmer on the tractor) not only fails to yield an adequate wage but is also a
symptom of cultural deprivation.

Nevertheless, "it may be dangerous to hazard too many generalizations
about the differences between those of Friel's stories that are set in Donegal
and those that are set in Tyrone or Derry."²⁹ Not everyone in Friel's Tyrone is
a settled member of society; not everybody in the Donegal hinterland is en-
dowed with a romanticized remoteness. The stories in general confirm
Tyrone Guthrie's view that "a close attachment to, and interpretation of, a
particular part of the earth is an absolute essential to any work of art which
can ever be of deep or lasting significance. It is one of the paradoxes of art that
a work can only be universal if it is rooted in a part of its creator which is most

privately and particularly himself. Such roots must sprout not only from the people but also the places which have meant most to him in his most impressionable years."[30] Friel's fictional world, however, only superficially embodies the degree of homogeneity Guthrie suggests. Moreover, Friel has successfully disguised his own presence in his world by placing in the forefront of the stories "the submerged population groups," which in Frank O'Connor's influential view denote a short story's typical social reality.[31] Friel's stories communicate a variety of submergences that are as much cultural and temperamental as they are economic or political.

They present, then, two zones, one broadly speaking the domain of nature, of the natural, the presocial or asocial, in man; the other, generally speaking, the social. Thus, as in the case of the actual terrain on which they draw, the stories may be crudely divided into two kinds which seem in direct contrast to each other. In fact, the stories and their zones complement each other. Together they add up to a world, since together they subscribe to an essential condition of any inhabitable place, variety. Just as, for all the topographical contrasts, there is a basic, indispensable continuity in the land between Omagh and the sea, Friel's stories exemplify difference and cohesion.

However convenient it may be to group the stories into nature-Donegal and social-Tyrone, it must be borne in mind that an arguably more important aspect of the stories is that they resist facile categorization. Their resistance to generalization is also a feature of their inner particularity. Ostensibly dealing with stereotypes and stock situations, these stories reveal a restlessness, loneliness, and frustration beneath their typically even-tempered surfaces.

The significance of nature can be readily appreciated from the title story of Friel's first collection. "The Saucer of Larks" tells of a visit to Donegal of two German civil servants whose job it is to locate the grave of a Luftwaffe pilot lost in action during World War II. The pilot has been given a decent burial by the locals who found his body. Now, however, it has been decreed that all German war dead in Ireland must be buried in a commemorative mass grave in County Wicklow, not very far from Dublin. To assist Herr Grass and his colleague, the local sergeant of police and his deputy, Guard Burke, act as guides to the pilot's grave, which is in a remote spot named Glennafushog, the larks' glen, "a miniature valley, a saucer of green grass bordered by yellow sand dunes" (*SOL*, 12) at the end of a promontory fronting the Atlantic ocean.

The trip takes place on a beautiful day, through what the sergeant refers to as "my kingdom . . . the best of creation" (*SOL*, 9). As the group proceeds farther into nature, the sergeant becomes increasingly susceptible to the sur-roundings, noting in particular their fitness as a last resting place: "Dammit, there's so much good life around you, you haven't a chance to be really dead!" (*SOL*, 10). But pleasure is modulated into more profound feeling, and light-hearted banter gives way to unspoken intimations of mortality, when they reach the saucer of larks. Their arrival is climaxed by an ascension of singing larks, performing in the natural amphitheater that is their home a hymn to life and to the departed: "The air was a great void of warmth around them. Gradually the emptiness was filled again by the larks." (*SOL*, 15).

The larks' performance is presented as a counterpoint to the sergeant's state of mind. He does not express his feelings directly, however: he commu-nicates them by asking Herr Grass to consider leaving the pilot in his perfect resting place. Herr Grass replies that such a possibility is unthinkable, and back in the familiarity of the barracks and his daily round the sergeant im-plicitly agrees: " 'I don't know a damn what came over me out there,' he said in a low voice, as if he were alone" (*SOL*, 17). Whatever it was, it denotes in the story a power, emanating from nature, sufficient to make the sergeant lapse from duty and glimpse areas of his makeup to which his social role can-not give access. In contrast to Herr Grass, who is not at all moved by what he sees or deflected for a moment from his sense of duty, the more the sergeant moves outside his daily round the more he is moved by the pulse of greater things. Considerations of life and death enter his consciousness to the extent that he is willing to overturn his professional code of impersonally obeying orders. At the same moment as the sergeant entertains such an idea, the his-torical casualty (the airman) is claimed, and nature is at its most expressive, the lift-off of larks acting as a confirmation of the spontaneous and unex-pected scope of the Sergeant's humanity. Yet, as the end of the story main-tains (and as the detached presence of Guard Burke and Herr Heinrich, Grass's colleague, underlines), the sergeant is alone in his intimations, so much so that he can hardly comprehend their significance.

A similarly restorative experience, with perhaps more permanent conse-quences, is felt by Joe, the protagonist of "Among the Ruins." This story is also set in Donegal, among what Joe refers to as "my hills" (*SOL*, 22), and again a trip provides the story's narrative basis, even though Joe has been re-luctant to accede to his wife's insistence that he take her and their two chil-dren back to see his rural birthplace.

His reluctance is understandable, since when they arrive they find the ruins of the story's title, not the homestead. In more general terms, physical evidence of the social unit which was Joe's family has given way to the purely natural features of the place. These stimulate Joe into recapturing the happiness of his childhood, the inexplicable laughter he and his sister shared. Yet when his own son, Peter, becomes lost in his own incomprehensible play, Joe treats the boy as violently as his own father treated similar breaches in discipline. The effect of that reaction, however, is to prompt Joe into appreciating his son's play: "The fact that Peter would never remember it was of no importance; it was his own possession now, his own happiness, this knowledge of a child's private joy" (*SOL*, 29).

As a result of this perception, Joe is enabled to repossess his own childhood and its naturalness, perhaps a more fundamental piece of psychic property than "my hills." Its acquisition crystallizes the story's undogmatic but deeply felt interdependence of human nature and its impersonal counterpart. The story fittingly concludes, therefore, with a moving, knowing sense on Joe's part of what the trip has vouchsafed: "The past did have meaning. It was neither reality nor dreams, neither today's patchy oaks nor the great woods of his boyhood. It was simply continuance, life repeating itself and surviving" (*SOL*, 30). The experience of naturalness acts as a precondition for thought. The function of thought is to secure an accommodation between self and world, and to heal the effects of divisions made by time while in the very act of fully acknowledging them.

A similar sense of continuity emerges from "The Wee Lake Beyond," again in the context of a father-and-son relationship. Here the independence asserted with typical adolescent surliness by the narrator's son evokes memories of comparable behavior by the narrator when he was an adolescent. This story's emphasis is more obviously psychological than that of "Among the Ruins." Once again, however, the mediating factor that facilitates awareness in the story is nature. The narrator's youthful break from his father, his petulant sally into a remoter area of their fishing holiday, the "wee lake" in which he catches sight of the great fish—"I never saw so big a fish in any Donegal lake before or since" (*GIS*, 76)—that is the mythical, irrepressible, elusive symbol of his new-found autonomy, all denote the pattern of connections between natural and human phenomena, and the expressive capacities their relationship attains in Friel's stories.

In "My Father and the Sergeant" the local hills are referred to as sources of wealth (*SOL*, 191). Their value, and that of Friel's overall use of the natural world, is that they do not provide a passive backdrop. Nature acts in the stories as an authorizing presence, enabling those who come in contact with it to recognize dimensions of themselves to which they might otherwise remain blind. The revelatory moments—epiphanies, to use a term minted by James Joyce[32]—give access to the unconditionally human, the human unmasked of its social conditioning. Nature's active presence—which is presumably what

Walter Allen has in mind when he commends "The Saucer of Larks" for placing us "in the presence of something like Wordsworth's natural piety"[33]—is commissioned by a seemingly natural, or fortuitous, or unplanned encounter.

Friel's characterization of nature as a further, relatively unexperienced dimension of the human is underlined in stories which use natural phenomena in a manner which is the reverse of spontaneous and fortuitous. These stories feature animals as the means of bringing about the degree of personal recognition necessary for life to attain "continuance." The animals in question—a bantam cock in "Ginger Hero," a racing pigeon in "The Widowhood System," a greyhound in "The Fawn Pup," greyhounds in "The Barney Game"—are devices intended, through training, to enable their owners to lay a firmer claim to their world than they otherwise can. Nature thus is anthropomorphized, adapted to a plan, domesticated, disciplined to direct its instinctual play toward specific, vaguely social ends.

The full implications of such adaptation are to be seen most clearly in "Ginger Hero." Here, as in the other animal stories, Friel reveals his knowledge of local culture: cock fighting and pigeon racing are endemic to Ulster, and the former is a pastime particularly favored in the province's border areas. As is often the case in Friel's stories, the central characters in "Ginger Hero" are conceived in terms of opposites and unities. Tom, the narrator, is an easy-going laborer and father of a large family. Billy, his partner, is his superior in most ways—decisive, Tom's immediate boss at work, handler and trainer of the champion bird which gives the story its title. In addition to being partners in the cock-fighting venture, the two are brothers-in-law: Tom is married to the nagging, fertile Min, while Billy and the ample, good-natured Annie are childless.

On one level, the story narrates the illustrious history of Ginger Hero's career, culminating with his victory over Colonel Robson's Tiger, a victory for which Ginger, alas, pays the ultimate price. This final victory is obviously important, not only because of the honor and glory which it earns Ginger, but also because it earns substantial winnings as well (cock fights being traditional occasions for illegal gambling). On another level, however, which comes fully to the fore when Ginger is in his death-throes, the fighting encourages a natural intimacy between Tom and Annie (the latter, being childless, is free to accompany the men to the fights). While Ginger is dying, Tom and Annie are making love. Soon afterwards, Billy and Annie start a new life in England, and eventually Tom receives news that they are expecting a child. Meanwhile, Tom's own marriage improves: due to Ginger's earnings, Min has opened a shop (named Ginger Hero) and is blooming.

Billy may be the one to discipline the bird; indeed, they seem to be of a feather, judging by the details of his description—he's a former "bantam-weight boxer" with "two tufts of bright ginger hair that sprouted from the top of his high cheekbones" (*GIS*, 168). It is clear also that Billy needs the violence of cock fighting and the fulfillment and absoluteness of victory. Tom, on the other hand, is the man for more tentative and accidental human tasks. He is much less implicated in the machismo of the enterprise; thus, fittingly, he adds a human dimension to it. Since it is not Tom's way to espouse the brutal, direct, do-or-die ethos by which Ginger offers Billy fulfillment, he emerges from the story as the character who lets natural instincts take their unforced, disarming course—a course that would be far less evident without the ostensibly distracting but ultimately clarifying presence of Ginger Hero.

It seems relevant to see "Ginger Hero" in these terms, specifically, in view of the assertion that Ginger's final fight "invokes the conflict between the English landowners and the Irish peasantry."[34] While it is true that both Tom and Billy work on Lord Downside's estate, this aspect of their lives seems to be mentioned in order to ground the characters. Billy is by far the more ardent aficionado, though he earns more than Tom. Just as "The Saucer of Larks" has a historical aspect, "Ginger Hero" has a socio-economic component. In both cases, material that could lend itself to conceptual analysis lies latent and underdeveloped, suggesting that Friel means to express solidarity with the image of the human that the story seems naturally to bring into being. It may be that the intense play of human emotions can have effects as lacerating as those inflicted by a cock on its opponent. But their mode of expression is not necessarily brutal and can be creative.

Similar issues are presented in "The Widowhood System," though because the approach is broader (featuring, for example, a couple of "rude mechanicals"[35] from the village of Mullaghduff) the outcome is less affecting. The system in question has been perfected by Harry, the pigeon fancier, and enjoins his would-be champion bird to sexual abstinence prior to a race in the belief that this will cultivate his homing instincts. It doesn't, any more than Harry's allegedly Mendelian breeding system has produced a champion. The verdict delivered on both systems by Harry's unprepossessing sidekicks is that they are "not natural" (*GIS*, 26).

The way Harry treats the girl next door, Judith Costigan, is not natural either. (As is "Ginger Hero," there is explicit paralleling between human and animal: Judith is "plump, smooth, hazel-eyed" [*GIS*, 14]. Again, the parallel is introduced to establish a conflict at a deeper level, a conflict between reason or "system" and instinct or "nature.") Only when he's had a few too many drinks is he capable of expressing affection for her. Judith permits herself to be taken for granted in this manner, but only up to a point. Unlike a pigeon, whose homing instincts, Harry explains, operate "as simple as if he was running on railway lines" (*GIS*, 21), Judith can't function with such a mechanical degree of consistency, as her response, "Lucky bird . . . lucky, lucky bird" (*GIS*, 22) indicates. When Judith departs from her predictable round amidst rumours that she may be thinking of emigrating, Harry realizes the inadequacy of his approach to her, a realization that coincides with his acceptance that his "widowhood system" for the pigeon has also been misconceived. Ultimately, the pigeon can only go its own way. Permitting this to be the case finds, for its reward, happiness with Judith.

The genial vein of "The Widowhood System" is also that of "The Fawn Pup" (the stories even share a minor character, Fusilier Lynch, a dilapidated sportsman), where the eponymous animal has been so carefully looked after that, on its first night out, it shames its owners by deviating from the track to be by their side. The dog's indiscipline, its having never learned, parallels its owner's exuberant outlook. The initial impulse to train the dog comes from the fact that the owner, a teacher, has an exaggerated belief in the capacities of his former pupils, a number of whom are engaged as trainers. The hoots of a derisive crowd at the track and the unwholesome condition of the track itself bespeak the state of local society. For a moment, this state's reality and the dog's failure dampen the teacher's spirits. Before the evening is over, however, "he was in good humour again" (*SOL*, 51), this impulsive, credulous nature undiminished by his exposure to elements more wordly wise, less playful, less puppyish than himself. Like the dog, the man has not succumbed to the ethos of the track and its mechanical race.

Things are rather more serious in "The Barney Game," where the non-human exemplars, the hounds and the hare, give piteous expression to the exploitative sport that Crispin, the insecure lawyer, plays with his good-natured slob of an uncle, Barney. It may be "all blood sports disgusted" Crispin (*GIS*, 106), but he is plainly unaware of how the phrase *blood sport* describes the way he treats his relative. And indeed, much as Crispin might wish to jettison the game ("He was sick of it all" [*GIS*, 111]) in favor of a more honest approach, when this approach is attempted, the quarry, uncle Barney, resents it: Barney needs the illusion that there is not a game as much as Crispin needs the hard cash which is the game's object. The relentless manner in which the hounds kill the hapless hare has the effect of confirming Crispin in his own game (surely Friel intends the reader to see the double meaning of *game* in this context): "After all these years it had now become part of his nature" (*GIS*, 114).

By doing so, the game has frayed the bonds of natural attachment that hold Crispin to Barney. Crispin cannot believe that his love for his uncle might be all Barney needs: Crispin has to have money too. As in the other stories where animals intervene, the capacity for doing the human thing in order to sustain relationships is seen problematically. The ulterior motive, ostensibly the enabling agent in these stories' various plans, schemes, and systems, turns out to have disabling results, usually because their initiators give human contrariness insufficient credit. The essentially unsystematic and unpredictable character of human behavior defines human nature in these stories. The point made about the protagonist's father in "The Fawn Pup"— "these were anomalies in his make-up that left him larger than any pigeonhole" (*SOL*, 41)—applies to all the protagonists of these stories.

Nature, however, in either animate or inanimate form, supplies the context in which this largeness may be perceived. The animal stories do not discriminate between the places in which this context appears: "The Fawn Pup" is set in and around Omagh, in County Tyrone (*SOL*, 41), "Ginger Hero" in Donegal, "The Barney Game" (unusually) in Coleraine (*GIS*, 104), County Derry. The stories of inanimate nature's influence are set in County Donegal. Place seems less relevant than what is revealed within it. The same may be said of character. Their names—Tom, Harry, Joe—may be as undistinguished as those of their locales. Yet it is from their virtual anonymity that their stories are made. The frailty, blindness, and imperfections that these characters reveal at the individual level are both revealed and relieved at the generalized level provided by natural contexts. D. E. S. Maxwell's observation about "Johnny and Mick" that "its representativeness depends upon its realizing a distinctive individual situation"[36] describes Friel's overall achievement in the nature stories.

One of the features of the nature stories is that they tend to deal with figures in a landscape, rather than figures in society. As Friel's social stories bear out, being in society means having an institutional life. In the nature stories, the characters' membership in institutions has either temporarily lapsed or has never been established. And in the social, or Tyrone, stories, the enlarging epiphanous moments nature vouchsafes are replaced as narrative objectives by instances of illusion and disillusion, confirming that society imposes constraints—constraints of duty, class, work, and family. Just as nature's epiphanies do not promise permanent enlargement, social constraints are not necessarily seen in an adverse light. The sergeant at the end of "The Saucer of Larks" implicitly wonders if he was not behaving in a deluded manner when asking the Germans to disobey orders, arguing for his dependence on the round of weekday duties that places him in a distinctive social role.[37] Nevertheless, a pattern of being blinded to the ways of the world and of coming to perceive such to be the case is discernible in those stories of Friel's which have an explicit, developed social setting. Moreover, this pattern has a reciprocal relationship to the nature stories. Thus, while in one sense Friel's fictional world appears to be a divided one, the complementary relationship between his family of nature stories and his family of social stories demonstrates its essential imaginative unity.

The theme of illusion is most fully and most satisfactorily treated in what has been called Friel's best story,[38] "Foundry House." Since childhood, Joe Brennan has been in awe of the Hogan family, foundry owners and inhabitants of the big house in whose gatelodge Joe grows up. Given the chance to return to the lodge, Joe accepts with alacrity and moves in with his large brood and genial, level-headed wife, who is rather less enamoured of the Hogans. The Hogan family has by this time grown up, and only the bedridden *pater familias*, Bernard, and his wife still live in Foundry House. A family reunion of sorts is in the offing, however, prompted by the arrival of a tape-recorded message from the daughter of the house, Claire, a nun in Africa. To play the message, Joe's expertise in matters electrical is required. He supplies the tape recorder and installs it.

Joe's expertise means much less to him, however, than the fact that it enables him to see the inside of Foundry House for the first time. What the reader sees is a state of total neglect: what Joe sees, however (as he tells his wife later), is "very nice," an untruth that is one of a tissue of misrepresentations about the events of the Hogan reunion. Thus, Joe does not describe the excruciating bathos of Claire's tape, nor does he reveal that at the sound of his daughter's voice old Bernard has an attack. He steadfastly maintains his claim that the Hogans are "a great, grand family." The story ends: "'The same as ever,' he crooned into the child's ear. 'A great family. A grand family'" (*SOL*, 67).

The presence of Joe's large family in the "chaotic" (*SOL*, 66) kitchen to which he returns after the reunion provides one of the main contrasts between his life and that of the Hogans. The Hogan children, Sister Claire and Father Declan, are obviously destined to remain childless. Their self-imposed condition of repressed fertility seems to be Foundry House's most obvious legacy, its version of "continuance." Joe cannot accept for what they are the ruins among which he finds himself, unlike his namesake in "Among the Ruins." But Joe's illusions of family grandeur are not based on his actual experience of the family. His halting speech in their company eloquently expresses his unease, his unconscious awareness of the extent of the cultural distance between them. What remains important to Joe is the idea of the family. The judgment that it is a story in which "the only true aristocrat is the imagination,"[39] points to Joe's latent, undemonstrative idealism.

In this light, the fact that both he and the Hogans are Catholics is noteworthy. As Catholics they are essentially detached from the larger context of the Northern Ireland state—the house is off "the main Belfast-Derry road" (*SOL*, 53)—and their religion ostensibly gives them common ground. The connection between Joe and the family, however, depends not on social enablement but on social disenfranchisement. Thus, it is only in his own mind that Joe can preserve and cherish the family's significance. His sense of the family is both real to Joe and disclaimed by the world upon which it is based. In other words, Joe's attachment to the Hogans is a real illusion, its very transparency articulating the layers of deprivation and obsolescence which Joe implicitly requires it to mask. It evokes sympathy for being so understandable in human terms, rather than condemnation for its social inadequacy.

The objective, disillusioning view of the Hogan family as a social institution seen over Joe's shoulder, so to speak, is the basis for Joe's subjective need to go on glorifying the family.[40] In "The Illusionists" there is a similar dispelling and reinstallation of illusion. The annual visit of M. L'Estrange, the magician, to the young narrator's school stimulates his desire to escape the narrow confines of school and home. It also stimulates his father, the schoolmaster and L'Estrange's host, to wax eloquent about putative professional achievement. The guest also is an eloquent praiser of his own past. The story focuses on the visit during which the two men, fueled as usual with whiskey, denounce each other's tall tales of glory. This does not deter the narrator from following through with his ambition to set out with L'Estrange. But this illusion of novelty and success is quickly dispelled. The child, having barely traveled beyond the first turn in the road, where he finds a drunk L'Estrange floundering, returns home disenchanted. By way of consoling the boy, his mother tenderly paints a verbal picture of all the bright days ahead in which the stuff of their daily lives are touched with an imaginative glow.

L'Estrange has been exposed for the "sham" and "fake" (*GIS*, 40) the mother has known him to be all along. The narrator's father has unmasked his pseudonymous claims to notoriety: "I know who you are, Monsieur illusionist L'Estrange: your real name's Barney O'Reilly" (*GIS*, 40). The boy himself has found the illusionist's theatricality to be wanting. L'Estrange's annual visit may be an overture of spring, as the story's opening sentence insinuates, but it is nothing like the real thing—nothing, that is, like "the great fun we'll have—oh dear God it'll be powerful—when the good weather comes" (*GIS*, 44). Immediately following those words of his mother, how-

ever, comes the narrator's acknowledgment that they too contain a necessary
illusion: "I stopped crying and smiled into her breast because every word she
said was true. But it wasn't because I remembered that it was true that I
believed her, but because she believed it herself, and because her certainty
convinced me" (GIS, 44). It is not the therapeutic powers of good weather
that is the point so much as the fact that the mind needs to ascribe such potential to a future that it cannot control. Once again, it is not the existence of
an illusion that articulates the story's substance, but the reality of and necessity for illusion.

The illusions that the illusionistic teacher-father cherishes about his professional achievements are matters of fact in the case of the teacher-father in
"My Father and the Sergeant." And perhaps as a corollary, the father in "The
Illusionists" cannot, or does not, give his son an alternative world by which he
might satisfy his imaginative longing, while the father who is also a "sergeant" devotes his professional life to directing the scholarship class (which
includes his narrator-son) to a wider world so that he will not "rot his life
away" (SOL, 191). The story examines the duality that its title expresses by
contrasting the father's ambitions with the pedagogical style of Paul
Desmond, hired as a substitute when the father falls ill.

The substitute's style is to dispense with the curriculum and appeal to the
pupils' imaginations. His is the soft spirit of romance: the sergeant is the stern
voice of reason. Yet, for all the eye-opening encounters with unfamiliar lore
that Desmond effects, he does not seem in control of his own romanticism.
His unstructured, institutionally subversive approach leads to his kissing
Maire, the narrator's beloved classmate, and a hasty, scandalous departure.
The sergeant leaves his sickbed to take over, and things in school revert to piti-
less drill, while the narrator is restored to Maire. Reality, comprising the necessary doubleness of discipline and love, has returned.

Yet such an outcome is not necessarily a critique of what Paul Desmond
provided. Rather it is a commentary on its insufficiency. More compelling,
according to the story, is the teacher-father's suppression of romance in the
classroom in the belief that this serves the purpose of the outside world—that
is, the world of Boards of Education, prestigious secondary schools and the
like: a world of complex social institutions, in fact. This is a world that has defeated the teacher-father; hence, for all his pedagogic gifts, his spending "the
whole of his restless life" in a "one-roomed building" (SOL, 182) in rural
County Tyrone.

It would be unkind to label as illusion the teacher's ambitions for his pupils. At the same time, however, that ambition has the same degree of psychological necessity and perfection of vision typical of the reality of illusion in

"Foundry House" and "The Illusionists." Once again, this story's central figure is characterized in terms of his poverty (which in this case is caused by the failure of his career to develop), and of the dignity with which he fashions the persona of "sergeant" to cope with his poverty. The fragility of such a creation is captured in the story's concluding vignette, in which the narrator, restored to things in their familiar arrangement, sounds as though this is the state in which he believes they will last. He doesn't know any better; hence has no need of a persona (or, rather, his narrator's persona does not influence the story's effect). The naive wish expresses the poignant desire.

The character of Desmond, and to a certain extent that of L'Estrange, brings to the fore an important type in Friel's social stories: the outsider, the interloper who unwittingly exposes or redefines the accepted codes and accommodations of the status quo. His influence in the social stories is comparable in its effect to that of animals in the nature stories, and his presence communicates a similarly complex ethos in which issues of freedom, discipline, and expressiveness are inconclusively but resonantly combined. The outstanding case in point is "The Diviner."[41]

This story deals with Nelly Devenny, a charwoman, who having made a disastrous marriage to an alcoholic, remarries after his death a man who to all appearances is "the essence of respectability" (*GIS*, 116). Nobody can be sure of this Mr. Doherty's credentials, however, since he is not from Nelly's village of Drumeen and is the opposite from being sociable. It turns out that appearances have been deceptive. When, after a boating accident at a local lake, Mr. Doherty's body is eventually recovered, his coat pockets are found to contain whiskey bottles. Nelly's illusion of respectability is shattered.

Her husband's body would never have been recovered without the intervention of the diviner, the story's most obvious outsider, summoned from afar to work his uncanny skills where more physical methods have failed. But the recovery of the body and the subsequent shock to Nelly's social standing is not all the diviner accomplishes. His detachment from Nelly's social world is a precondition for her being detached from the status her new husband had almost brought her: "Hers . . . were not only the tears for twenty-five years of humility and mortification but, more bitter still, tears for the past three months, when appearances had almost won, when a foothold on respectability had almost been established" (*GIS*, 127–28).

Nelly's social loss, in turn, seems an act of divination, raising to the surface assumptions about the village of Drumeen and its social codes. The story concludes with prayers being said for the soul of the departed, a gesture that highlights how little Christian charity is being extended to his widow. In this context, Nelly's illusion of respectability is a more significant model of integrity than that suggested by the institutionalized response generated by the local priest. As for the diviner, his impersonal, pragmatic contribution has created ripples on the surface of Drumeen for which nobody is either willing or equipped to take moral responsibility. His arrival denotes the latent capacity for revelation that lies beneath the commonplace. It might even be thought that the diviner is, like L'Estrange and Paul Desmond (whose real vocation is painting), an artist manqué.

The role of the priest in "The Diviner" (and the possibility that the story's title may be a sly pun on the priest's calling) underlines the generally adverse social contributions made by the Catholic clergy in Friel's social stories. A priest is responsible for the shape assumed by the teaching career of the narrator's father in "My Father and the Sergeant." Clerical attitudes are seen at a disadvantage in the matter of the burial of the narrator's Uncle Cormac, the eponymous outsider in "The Death of a Scientific Humanist." In "The First of My Sins" the child-narrator's first confessor ratifies the rapid withdrawal of adult sympathy from Uncle George, whose petty thievery the narrator has betrayed. The result is the narrator's realization that it is with the outsider that his own sympathies lie, not with the moral structures that support those institutions seeking to define the scope and play of those sympathies, Church and family. And when spurned, outlandish Grandfather wants to embarrass the narrator's mother in "My True Kinsman"; he ironically inveighs against her religious punctiliousness: "Not off to confession, again, daughter-in-law? Heavens, woman, but you must lead a profligate life!" (SOL, 70).

"My True Kinsman" is a vivid example of how an outsider's presence reveals the confines of those institutions of which he is not a member. And the narrator's decision to give his grandfather the money meant to buy iodine for a minor injury incurred by his mother is clearly a decisive moment in his development. Not surprisingly, it comes on his tenth birthday. In addition, the money may be seen to be far less valuable than what the grandfather provides, a cultural tour of the village of Mullaghduff, with a commentary delivered in "wonderful words" (SOL, 75). Naturally and spontaneously—which in this case means, unprompted by the dictates of an institution—the youngster allows himself to be taken under the maverick's wing. The shelter from the rain provided by the coat his grandfather loans him for his return home is a reciprocal gesture—spontaneous and winningly improvident. The coat's smell, previously found menacing, now exerts a talismanic force on the child: "The smell was through me and all about me. And I knew that as long as it lasted, I would have the courage to meet my mother and tell her the terrible news—that I had no iodine and no money and that Grandfather had got me" (*SOL*, 78). Ultimately, however, this state of affairs has come about because at some level the narrator wanted it. Whatever label may be attached to this level—individualistic, rebellious, cultural—it exists in counterpoint to the mother's decorous, institutional orientation. Acquaintance with it enlarges the child's sense of the knowable, gives him scope to fantasize, adds color to staidness, and not only justifies the existence of outsider figures but ratifies the basis of illusion. For, as the social stories collectively state, the reality of illusion is the human need for and acceptance of alternatives.

Friel's stories have been criticized on the grounds that the author, "by refusing to test or breach the social and moral premises of the rural area in which his stories are set, is in danger of confining his work within a regionalist framework."[42] The stories surmount this risk by embracing it. Their regionalist framework is the basis and core of their achievement, a source of enablement rather than of disenfranchisement. Friel has produced in the stories a literature appropriate to its world of origin and as a result has created a world indeed.

The basis of this world is its integrity. An overview of the stories reveals how the County Tyrone pieces function as a commentary on their County Donegal neighbors, and vice versa. Supplementing this generalized standpoint is a sense that nature provides what society is deficient in. Nature offers instances of detachment, escape, illumination, and perspective. It confers on its unsuspecting visitors the unsettling and enriching otherness of its presence. In animal form nature passively provides a focus that unobtrusively highlights the narrative material's human dimension. What social life represses, nature sustains, as the sexual aspect of "Ginger Hero," "The Widowhood System," and "The Wee Lake Beyond" illustrates. Thus, while it may be that "the vibrant solidity of settings is perhaps the strongest single impression left by the world of the stories,"[43] it is difficult to overlook the characters who occupy the foreground of these settings and who, for all their failings, render the settings significant. It is Friel's people who occasion nature's amenability to discourse, thereby humanizing it.

Ultimately, however, people do not belong within the otherness of nature. Joe goes home with his family from the ruins of his childhood home; Tom and Min patch up their marriage by means of a familiar rural institution, the little shop. People belong with their own kind. Society offers the possibility of community and a refuge from what Pascal has called "the eternal silence of those infinite spaces."[44] In particular, the family offers shelter from the uncertainties of a seductive but unknowable wider world. So the boys in "My Father and the Sergeant" and "The Illusionists" discover. For adults, their hope is to drown the menacing silence. Hence the commitment of "the Sergeant" and old Con's insistence on the reality of buried treasure in "The Gold in the Sea": they mean to be saviors.

Thus, while nature and society are distinct environments in Friel's stories, their distinctiveness is less important, finally, than the fact that they are not opposed. Rather, they are understood to be equally revealing and instructive manifestations of what the world at large contains and are presented as alternative, complementary perspectives on the human continuum ("life repeating itself and surviving"). The success of the stories, taken as a whole, is to a considerable extent their gentle but insistent representation of reciprocity and compatibility between what might conventionally be considered irreconcilable categories—reality and illusion, nature and society, mountains and men.

Such harmony may also be found in other aspects of Friel's fiction. Thus the stories preserve the geographical reality of their origins as well as being at the same time imaginative transmutations of that reality: rural names, such as "the townland of Knockenagh" (*SOL*, 182) in "My Father and the Sergeant" have been invented, but the country—"a shelf of arable land buttressing the face of grey-black mountains that keep County Tyrone from County Donegal" (*SOL*, 182)—is real.

Another, more delicate, example of the reciprocity between absence and presence in Friel's stories is the character of the author himself. It is through his self-effacement that we become aware of him. Rather than fill the role of author as authority-figure, Friel obviates his own controlling interest in events, preferring to share the essential passivity of his subjects. As a result the stories seem to take their own shape, in their own time. Their evolution is articulated through the formation of delicate networks of implication and resonance. The author's supple patterning of general context and individual case, of details that are matches and details that are equally illuminating mismatches, is one of the principle disciplines of these stories that a theme-seeking, schematic reading is liable to overlook. And as though to authenticate their being underwritten, the stories lack overt drama, and potentially dramatic incidents expressly lack dramatic responses on the part of those affected by them (Nelly's private, unstaunchable tears at the end of "The Diviner" is a particularly moving case in point). It is this very lack of clamor, either in language or in plot, that enables the reader to hear the key in which Friel's plainsong renders, in Seamus Heaney's phrase, "the music of what happens."[45]

In his stories Friel has created an imaginatively integrated replica of the world of his early years. To require that the stories function as an interpretation of that world and "breach" its "premises" (as though it were a world under siege) is to risk misrepresenting the spirit of Friel's fiction. Friel's cre-

ation speaks not only to literature or in the idiom of literary criticism, it also
addresses the world that is its origin and to which it has remained faithful in
its fashion. Thus, while it is extremely doubtful that Friel wrote his stories to
repudiate Winston Churchill's dismissal of "the dreary steeples of Tyrone
and Fermanagh,"[46] it must be counted among his stories' achievements that
they effect such a repudiation. The stories rehabilitate the alleged "dreari-
ness" not by disguising it but by revealing it, by seeing in it an opportunity for
honesty rather than a reason for rejection. In Seamus Deane's words: "The
narrowness of the social life is bitter, but the complexity of the moral life
within is generous."[47]

It is in the context of such loyalty to a world—a loyalty that is reproduced
at the artistic level by the stories' many-sided integrity and urge to harmony—that the question of the Border in Friel's work may be considered.
Rather than being invisible or having no effect on Friel's work, the Border between the North of Ireland and the Irish Republic makes a distinctive imaginative contribution to it. The stories implicitly accept the existence of a
Border in the distinction they make between County Tyrone and County
Donegal. But they also transcend that distinction by establishing reciprocal
relationships between those two territories. Imaginative geography super-
cedes historical actuality.

To Friel the writer the Border is a word, a concept, a code, a criterion as
palpable and invisible as any other cultural condition. As such, it does not
exist in the world of his characters as a visible, objective, historical entity; it
is a defining characteristic of their world that has been absorbed into the
fabric of their lives. Friel's imaginative transmutation of geographical reality has effectively sublimated the Border as a physical entity. It has also allowed him, however, to insinuate the idea of the Border. Thus Friel has
denied himself explicit mention of the Border so as to be imaginatively free
to communicate its ethos.

Friel's characters, on the other hand, occupy positions that connote the
opposite of such freedom. They are defined by constraint, limitation, and
incompleteness. The majority of them are virtually anonymous. They experience various kinds of social marginalization. They are almost invaria-
bly Catholics, but neither their faith nor its institutions enlarge or
alleviate their condition. Awareness of a wider world and a larger life
comes from beyond the ambit of their daily round and through unfamiliar agents, human and otherwise. These agents, delegates of the absence
at the center of the protagonists' lives, offer means of making deficiency
admissable and containable.

In order to install those means firmly within the protagonists' narrow world, the need to cross borders must be articulated. Typically, Friel proposes no one way of articulating the need of making the crossing. In "The Saucer of Larks" the sergeant is obliged to consider an alternative to dutiful obedience. Tom breaks the barrier of marital fidelity in "Ginger Hero," a triumph more worthy of his humanity than any made by the fighting cock. The narrator of "My Father and the Sergeant" allows Paul Desmond's influence: that enables him to live more securely than ever in his father's world. The alternative world—the world which the Border declines to admit—is the world that completes the actual world.

The willingness exhibited by Friel's protagonists to extend themselves in either thought or deed suggests their capacity to find the outsider in themselves, to inhabit a more natural and more complete edition of themselves than their restrictive, Border-haunted society can tolerate. Without borders there can be no outsiders. But without outsiders there is no alternative, there is no freedom to encounter an alternative. The spirit of freedom is what finally imbues the world of Friel's stories. It is this spirit that the reciprocity and harmony of his fictional world, considered as a totality, underwrite. (It is also this spirit, considered problematically, that animates Friel's plays.) Like so many other features of Friel's work, however, freedom has a dual character. By allowing his characters the freedom to exist defined by their own border mentality and that of their society he locates them precisely in geographical reality. They are real by virtue of their distinctiveness. Free to encounter alternatives to their restrictions, they inhabit imaginative geography. Thus they lapse out of their limitations and become unconditionally human.

From Storyteller to Playwright

The republication of Friel's stories in *The Saucer of Larks: Stories of Ireland* (1969), *Selected Stories* (1979), and *The Diviner* (1983) has kept the author's reputation as a writer of stories alive long after he abandoned the form. Yet the finality with which the appearance of his second volume of stories, *The Gold in the Sea*, ends the story-writing phase of his career is somewhat deceptive. Friel abandoned the form, but remained faithful to the world of the stories. Indeed, his adoption of the theater could be interpreted as a clarification and a public avowal of that fidelity. Rather than denoting a discrete creative period, subsequently marginalized by his playwrighting success, the stories are a seedbed for Friel's theatre. The claim that there is an intimate, though by no means totally congruent, relationship between Friel's stories and his plays offers a means of presenting a preliminary description of the integrity of Friel's imaginative terrain and the development of his artistic vision of it.

Superficial connections between the stories and the plays are plainly evident. The issue of capitation—the educational authorities' ruling that schools will be staffed and funded according to the number of pupils attending them—is the basis of the tense dynamic of autonomy and social structure in "My Father and the Sergeant"; it is also the basis of the plot in Friel's second play for radio, *To This Hard House*. The threnodial litanies of locales in two of Friel's most celebrated plays, *Faith Healer* and *Translations*, evoke the more private but equally expressive round of postings to which Mrs. Burke subjects herself and her husband in "The Flower of Kiltymore": "from Kiltymore to Culdreivne, from Culdreivne to Ballybeg, from Ballybeg to Beannafreaghan, from Beannafreaghan back to Kiltymore" (*GIS*, 133–34). The linguistic difficulties experienced by the sergeant in "The Saucer of Larks" anticipates *Translations* by being a subtle metaphor for the more elusive incompatibilities of ethos within whose framework the story takes shape.

In addition, and less trivially, two of Friel's plays are based on short stories. Reworked, "The Highwayman and the Saint" from *The Gold in the Sea* becomes *Losers* in the dramatic diptych *Lovers: Winners and Losers*. The differences between the basic ingredients of both story and play—cast of characters, plot, and denoument—are negligible; in both cases, the protagonist is the victim of an unholy alliance between religiosity and its moral soulmate, hypocrisy. Yet, the two pieces are decisively distinct due to the nonnaturalistic devices that give dramatic force and point to the play. By disturbing the rather naive chronological development of "The Highwayman and the Saint" the play brings to the fore the material's inner reality. *Losers* presents a series of tableaux depicting the completeness of the protagonist's defeated condition. "The Highwayman and the Saint," however, does not succeed in overcoming the material's anecdotal novelty. (As will be discussed below, *Losers* also gains in scope from being presented in the context of a diptych.) Thus, without making extravagant claims for *Losers*—in fact, *Lovers: Winners and Losers* is not in the first rank of Friel's plays—a comparison of the play with its original demonstrates both Friel's continuing thematic and geographical loyalty to his world and the degree to which his artistic possession of that world is enhanced by the sense of presence, projection, and completeness of effect that the theater provides.

The other adaptation of material from page to stage is a more graphic illustration of the principle of fidelity and departure generally articulated in the relationship between Friel's stories and plays. "Foundry House" is more substantial, and so is the play in which it is recast, *Aristocrats*.[48] The relationship between the two pieces is illustrated by the story's most important scene, in which old Bernard Hogan's disabled condition takes a turn for the worse when hearing the tape-recorded voice of his daughter. The same scene acts as a turning point in *Aristocrats*, and to describe it as a turning point is to isolate the fundamental difference between the dramatic scene and its fictional counterpart.

In "Foundry House" the scene makes no difference either to the condition of the Hogan family or to the illusions of faithful Joe. The fact that old Mr. Hogan merely sinks further toward his end, without meeting it, underlines the essentially unchanging nature of things for all concerned. "Father" in *Aristocrats*, on the other hand, dies as a result of hearing his daughter's voice on tape, thereby releasing the rest of the family and its retainers into a more complex, more decisive, and more independent sense of who they are and what now they might do with their lives. If, as Seamus Deane has said, "the only true aristocrat" in "Foundry House" is "the imagination," the achievement of the reworked material is to dignify the anachronistic aristocrats by endowing them with a reality principle. Not all the characters share this principle, or share it completely, but this does not invalidate it.

The revolution in perception indicated by a comparison between "Foundry House" and *Aristocrats* has a more general application when Friel's plays are considered in the light of his stories. Like many of Friel's stories and plays, both "Foundry House" and *Aristocrats* deal with families. Many of the families in the plays, however, lack the completeness of structure that the families in the stories possess. Partly due to the necessarily restricted child's-eye-view that communicates Friel's typical narrative perspective on them, families in the stories are generally seen as detached, discrete entities, tangentially if decisively connected to social structures more powerful than themselves. The plays, however, offer a different, more problematic sense of families.

A convenient way in which to outline the change—a change that exemplifies Friel's imaginative development—is to consider the relative status of mothers in the stories and in the plays. Broadly speaking, the stories have mothers, the plays do not. The role of the mother in, for example, "The Illusionists" makes her the voice of duty and practicality, bidding her son to attend to the chores instead of listening to the pair of male gasbags who drunkenly attempt to outdo each other with fantasies of rich pasts. Yet she is the voice also of containable illusion, encouraging the child to picture the year ahead, thereby implicitly easing the burden of the present. Thus, perhaps unwittingly, she participates, though in quietist and putatively realistic terms, in the activity of the two hopeless men. This power of influencing the child-narrator's conflicts, mollifying him by setting them in a continuum, is also evident in "The Death of a Scientific Humanist." And while this regulatory office is not confined to mothers—as is borne out by, for example, old Con in "The Gold in the Sea"—it is more typical of mothers' behavior than it is of any other Friel character type. Therefore, the absence of mothers in the plays means the absence of a character who, in the stories, had a powerful integrative influence on the family—a presence that can keep the family more or less immune from the threat of other, more worldly, influences. So central is such a presence in the stories that it is possible to devote works—"My True Kinsman" and "The First of My Sins"—to accommodating alternative presences by which mothers might be challenged.

Perhaps because the plays cannot present a child's-eye-view it is impossible for them to ratify the gently ironic interplay between the reality of innocence and the illusion of safety that sounds the note of typicality in many of Friel's family, child-centered stories. In any case, the absence of such material from the plays seems consistent with the absence of mothers, and in turn these absences are consistent with deficient fathers, fragmented families, and the world at large flooding in upon indefensible homes. Friel's rejection of mother figures results in the family being considered more problematically in his work. The playwright's disinclination to be loyal to one of the crucial figures from the world of the stories results in dramas where family and other types of loyalty becomes a vital issue. A revealing reflection of this development is that while in plays such as *The Gentle Island* and *Living Quarters* natural families prove to be untenable, murderous institutions, plays like *The Freedom of the City* and *Volunteers* reconstitute a sense of family—replete with the pride, solidarity, and fondness for ritual long thought to be sources of cohesiveness in the natural family—from characters thrown together either by force of historical circumstances or for some other impersonal reason. Friel's reexamination of the family as an imaginative resource provides another striking illustration of the way in which the plays are both related to, and developments of, the stories.[49]

Similar observations may be made about the plays' use of place. The geographical reality of the stories is once again evoked in the plays. The wild young woman described as the mother of Gar O'Donnell, protagonist of *Philadelphia, Here I Come!*, seems to be from the same family as the narrator's granny in "Mr. Sing My Heart's Delight": "She was small—and wild and young—from a place called Bailtefree beyond the mountains; and her eyes were bright, and her hair was loose, and she carried her shoes under her arm until she came to the edge of the village."[50] And both of them may well be blood relations of the eponymous heroine of "Aunt Maggie, the Strong One" (*SOL*, 122–32). Not all the plays are set in northwest Ulster, but there

is a sense of hinterland in those that are that is quite as palpable as that provided by the natural settings of the stories. The big difference, however, is
that virtually all the plays set in Friel country are set in Ballybeg. An anglicization of the Irish *baile beag* (small town), the name connotes a generic, archetypal, small, remote, rural community. In Ulf Dantanus's words: "In its
social, economic and religious characteristics, in its implied political history,
the village of Ballybeg is emblematic of Ireland and a part of Ireland rather
than any one specific village in that area. In this respect Ballybeg represents
an effort, on Friel's part, at the wider application of a place, towards some
kind of local universality."[51]

Regardless of this seemingly paradoxical intention, Friel has managed by
creating Ballybeg to compress into one social and geographical entity the
sense of place that is diversified throughout the stories. One of the effects of
this act of compression is to render redundant purely topographical accuracy.
The temptation of facile picturesqueness is resisted as completely as the
temptation of easy sentimentality that mothers present. In addition, the crystallization of place that the invention of Ballybeg achieves means that nature
is no longer available as the *lieu theatrale* of insight, as it had been in, for example, "The Saucer of Larks." The role of nature is supplanted in the plays by
that of culture.

This development does not mean that the characters in the plays are particularly cultured, at least not in the sense of high culture. In fact, those relatively few dramatic characters conversant with the classics—Hugh and
Jimmy in *Translations*, Trilbe Costello and Mr. Ingram in *The Loves of Cass
McGuire*—are just as doomed and deluded as those without learning. Culture, rather, should be understood as a vivid matrix of clichés, traditions, historical conditionings and misprisions, intellectual formulations, prejudices,
and attachments that in the unevenness and contradictoriness of their interaction enact codes of affiliation between person and place in Friel's plays.[52]

As nature did in the stories, culture in the plays offers a context in which
the distinct and solitary promptings of individuality may be experienced and
reflected. Nature is a model of continuity whose counterpart is inescapability.
It is a tissue of properties communally available but appropriated and utilized primarily by means of individual perception. Nature is the world without man, in which man can find reflections of himself. Similarly, culture
offers models of continuity and collectivity. For Friel it provides a common
mind-set which can both provide an identity to those who share it and constrain that identity's freedom and autonomy. Thus culture, being exclusively
the work of man—being, in effect, the world according to man—offers a
more complex, more focused, more condensed optic through which issues

concerning self and world may be perceived. It will be seen that culture as a source of drama is one of Friel's enduring preoccupations as a playwright, present in plays as different from each other as *Philadelphia, Here I Come!*, *Volunteers*, and *Translations*, to mention only three very obvious cases in point. As though to maintain a link between the stories and that area of the plays that seems most distinct from them, however, Friel makes the character who is most resourceful, culturally speaking, take the role of outsider, as he did in the stories. And as in the stories, this character is most adept at changing roles, accents, and demeanors—at being theatrical, in fact.[53]

As though to confirm the salience of culture in the plays, language, culture's primary instrument, occupies a much more prominent place in Friel's theater than it did in the stories. In fact, language itself—its duplicities and resilience, its essential play—becomes one of the plays' subsidiary subjects. In general, there is greater verbal exuberance in the plays, an unexpected penchant for broad jokes, a marked increase in declaration and assertion, an obviously greater trust in conversation as an expressive device. The comparative paucity and generally nonproductive nature of conversation in the stories speaks eloquently of their protagonists' isolation. In the plays, however, the typical protagonist is inevitably a man of language, composing and recomposing his identity in the light of the cultural options to which his language provides access. Such activity does not necessarily cure the protagonist's isolation, but it does ensure that he is no longer the passive figure in a landscape typical of the stories.

The relationship between Friel's stories and plays, then, is complex and deep. On the one hand, it is clear that Friel's plays demonstrate how much he has rethought and outgrown the artistic origins revealed by the stories. The opportunities afforded by drama for both definitiveness of presentation and variety of approach to his material were clearly welcomed, and the material itself began to reveal nuances and potentialities of which the stories give little or no clue. Friel in his plays is a much more obviously individuated writer, intellectually committed and aesthetically adventurous to such a degree as to suggest that the theater was an artistic rebirth for him.

On the other hand, these advances are still very much in the service of the world of the stories, the modest characters who inhabit it, and the recessive culture that distinguishes and stigmatizes it. Moreover, Friel's development as a writer has not compromised the fundamental humanity that graces all of his work, and of which the stories remain the first, and not necessarily least, revealing articulation.

Chapter Two
The Road to Philadelphia

Friel began writing plays while his story-writing career was in its prime. His first plays were produced in 1958, four years before his first collection of stories was published and two years before he left teaching to write full-time. Yet, given the technical accomplishment of and international audience for the stories, the choice of a new medium and its different demands may seem, on the face of it, perverse—particularly in the light of Friel's admission that "I am not aware that I have any theatrical pedigree."[1] Compared to his stories, Friel's early plays are awkward in execution. Moreover, plays in general are typically premised on the assumption that action and language contain a dynamic expressiveness by means of which the dramatic enterprise attains reality. The character of this reality, generally speaking, denotes decisiveness, change, and definitive activity. In contrast, Friel's stories are premised on quiescence being as expressive as action, on silence being as revealing as speech, and on decisiveness being a remote option.

Additionally, and by way of partially explaining Friel's lack of theatrical credentials, the theater in Ulster has largely meant the theater in Belfast.[2] D. E. S. Maxwell reports that "a 'little theatre' begun in Derry in the late 1940s languished and soon foundered,"[3] which suggests that the Ulster hinterland, in Friel's formative years, did not possess the cultural self-confidence to sustain its own theatrical life. (The establishment of Field Day expresses both a claim to such self-confidence and the novelty of the claim.) Such a lack of stimulating models and criteria raise the possibility that Friel's commitment to drama may have been made for cultural and intellectual reasons, or for reasons of artistic integrity, rather than because, as a developing writer, he was in the right place at the right time. Indeed, it would be entirely consistent with Friel's career as a playwright to find that he embarked on this career because the theatre is "the most democratic of the arts."[4]

Radio Days

It is hardly likely that Friel chose radio drama for his first pieces of theater because Guthrie had pioneered the form for the British Broadcasting Corporation (BBC) in Belfast during the 1920s. Lack of local opportunity and remoteness from the theatrical worlds of Belfast and Dublin (not to mention London) encouraged him to use the medium most conveniently available. Doing so did not necessarily mean indifferent productions of inferior material. The radio play as a form, however, has an illustrious European pedigree. Many state and semistate radio systems in Europe have sophisticated production values and ambitious cultural commitments.[5] The medium has commanded the attention of artists as aesthetically fastidious as Samuel Beckett. And Friel would no doubt have been aware of the impressive contributions made to radio drama by the Ulster poet Louis MacNeice.

Friel's work for radio lacks MacNeice's poetry and Beckett's idiosyncracy, and indeed is not particularly distinguished by any standards. These plays represent, rather, his first, rather faltering steps in drama. Their closeness to the stories in theme and language is perhaps inevitable; Friel could hardly be expected to change his material in order to explore the new form. And while the early plays—*A Sort of Freedom, To This Hard House, A Doubtful Paradise*, and (to some extent) *The Blind Mice*[6]—belong in theme and language to the world of the stories, they also reveal modifications of that world.

The settings of *A Sort of Freedom, To This Hard House*, and *A Doubtful Paradise* has a more urban character than any found in the stories. The protagonists are more vividly and pressingly connected to a world of work. Their plots also debate questions regarding the public and private ethics that work generates. In other words, these plays contain a more obvious social orientation than Friel's most socially inclined stories. The result is the presence of a more critical, more argumentative, more confrontational atmosphere in the plays. The plays also express a more explicit sense of defeat and hopelessness among those who come into conflict with social institutions than may be found in the stories. On the other hand, this development in intensity, and slight enlargement of thematic range, is not matched by comparable developments in language. And, as in the stories, verbal constraint denotes limitations of consciousness and an underdeveloped sense of individuality on the part of the plays' protagonists.

While *A Doubtful Paradise* and *The Blind Mice* have been included with Friel's radio plays, it is important to bear in mind that both were originally written for the stage, *A Doubtful Paradise* having the original title of *The Francophile*. As stage plays, they represent Friel's readiness to overcome the limitations of radio drama. Their lack of success on the stage and the author's decision to adapt them for radio make it appropriate to consider them as part of Friel's work for the latter medium.

The significance of *A Doubtful Paradise* and *The Blind Mice* derives not only from their relative artistic merits but from the fact that they underline both Friel's willingness to develop as a playwright and the tentativeness of that willingness in its early stages. His comparatively unpromising and certainly undramatic arrival as a playwright, however, has to be seen in the context of later developments. Within three years of *The Blind Mice* being produced on stage, *Philadelphia, Here I Come!* was playing on Broadway, Friel had an international hit on his hands, and his name attained a prominence which it has never subsequently relinquished, even if the reasons for that prominence have changed. As already mentioned, Friel has attributed the success of *Philadelphia* to the mentorship of Tyrone Guthrie. Yet the success of that play may also be seen as the culmination of the hard, self-taught lessons of the earlier plays, an examination of which is a portrait of Friel, playwright in the making.

A Sort of Freedom

Friel's first play, *A Sort of Freedom*, was produced by the BBC Northern Ireland Home Service and broadcast on 16 January 1958. Thus it was not offered to audiences outside Northern Ireland. It is based on a familiar and fundamental dramatic scenario, a study in contrasts. The contrast here is between Jack Frazer, owner of a trucking company, and his faithful employee of over twenty years, Joe Reddin. Change faces Frazer's company—much to his disgust, since it comes in the form of the unionization of the work force. The only resistance to this change in employer-employee relations comes from Joe Reddin, who insists on his freedom not to join. (As though to reinforce the isolation of Joe's position, his son is a militant union man. In keeping with the play's rather loose construction, however, the son's activities do not directly impinge on the father's stand.)

Change, though of a more positive kind, has also entered Frazer's private life. After years of childlessness, he and his wife have adopted a son. This change is also circumscribed by a subjective conception of freedom, in this case Frazer's irrational refusal to have his infant son immunized against tuberculosis, even though the law of the land requires him to do so. In contrast, no law obliges Joe to join the union.

The plot, such as it is, develops deteriorating relations between Frazer and the union because of Joe's intransigence, and parallels this development with Frazer's attempts to persuade the local doctor to sign forms falsely declaring the child to be immunized. His grounds for doing so echo Joe's assertion of freedom: "There's no freedom in a thing like that [immunization]. They should let every parent do as they want."[7] The doctor ironically mocks this

sentiment: "Bravo! . . . I propose a toast to 'The individual versus the State'"
(29). From Frazer's crass, antisocial egotism it is easy to see why he has been
called "a mean-spirited piece of work."[8] His nastiness is not confined to, or
best exemplified by, his attitude to immunization, since he eventually
complies with public health law. He shows no such compunction toward
faithful Joe, however, whose years of loyal service are sacrificed to business
expediency.

By a crude and rather dogmatic irony, the firing of Joe coincides with news
that Frazer's immunized son has succumbed to Sudden Infant Death Syn-
drome. The fruits of freedom are impossibly bitter. Yet Joe, hapless victim of
his own ideals when "this is not a world of ideals" (8), cannot see what has become of him. Betrayed and out of work, he continues to insist: "I still have my
freedom to do and say as I want . . . I'm a free man" (46). His wife's skeptical
reaction to this boast is as nothing compared to the audience's. The childish-
ness of Joe's view makes him seem a plaything of Frazer, and the logic of the
play's parallel structure implies that his social eclipse is as terminal in its own
way as the infant's. In any case, neither Joe nor Frazer's son have a future.
This condition, *pace* Joe, is confirmed rather than contradicted by Frazer's
derisory cash gift, given to ease their separation.

Such matters as public health policy, labor union activity, and a trucking
company provide *A Sort of Freedom* with a sense of social activity rather more
explicit than that found in the stories. Here there is a clear delineation of institutional obligation, of collectivity and social participation and their ethical
implications. There is also a backdrop of productivity and organization, and
of the characters existing in a man-made world. Public life has its private
counterpart, however, and it is in this realm that the substantial action of the
play takes place. The realm is ostensibly denoted by the family life of Frazer
and Reddin. Families, though, are not an integrated feature of the play, but
are simply a medium through which the more essential characterization is
transmitted. Private life in *A Sort of Freedom* is synonymous with the con-
sciences of the two main characters—or rather, the fact that Joe possesses a
conscience and Frazer does not.

The latter's deficiency is perfectly illustrated by the fact that, persuaded by
his wife to give Reddin a parting bonus, he reduces substantially the amount
that they agreed Joe should receive. Clearly, Frazer is free to behave in this
manner: this is the sort of freedom he exercises when he fires Joe. But it is a
freedom of such an absolute kind that it degrades its exponent and corrodes
those exposed to it (who, along with Joe, include Mrs. Frazer and their infant
son). It is the sort of freedom that, according to the play, finds expression in a
loveless, issueless marriage and in loyalty opportunistically betrayed.

Frazer's payment, ironically, is for Joe the final proof of his former employer's good faith. As such, it is the play's ultimate demonstration of this character's capacity for self-delusion. The primary evidence of this capacity is Joe's claim to freedom, since freedom is hardly what working for Frazer denotes. Joe's limitations are the equal and opposite of Frazer's. They arise from an excess of conscience, from conscience informed by uncritical naiveté, and thus are incapable of telling him where his best social interest lies. Joe is perfectly at liberty to live in the blinding light of such loyalty to principle. But it is a loyalty that finds expression in family fragmentation and in the prospect of economic disenfranchisement.

In some respects, Joe Reddin recalls Joe Brennan of "Foundry House"—in his loyalty, in his reluctance to question, and in his blinkering idealizations. Joe Brennan, though, is not a social victim because of his delusions. His job makes him quite independent of the Hogans. His attachment to them is a less compromised embodiment of freedom. In *A Sort of Freedom*, however, there seems to be a direct correlation between an increased emphasis on social conditions and a more explicit degree of social—indeed, moral—eclipse. Joe's refusal to see his own demoralization is consistent with his behavior throughout the play. From such consistency the play milks an unpalatable mix of defeat and disillusion. To say that "The ending is ironic, discomforting"[9] is something of an understatement.

To This Hard House

Friel's second play, *To This Hard House*, was produced soon after his first, on 24 April 1958, and again was broadcast for local consumption by the BBC Northern Ireland Home Service.

This play depicts the plight of Daniel Stone, a teacher who has spent most of his career running a small country school and who late in life learns that because of declining student numbers his school will close. His plight consists of his inability to see the writing on the wall, and his decline through the play is awkwardly accompanied by a deterioration of his sight. To some extent, however, his failure is not, in the first instance, entirely his own fault.

The play opens with a visit from Blackley, an official from the Ministry of Education, who reassures Stone that, all things being equal, Meenbanid school will remain open. All things do not remain equal, of course—families prefer the new school, and new social opportunities generally, in Clareford, as does Stone's only colleague Judy Flanagan. In one sense, therefore, Stone is a casualty of change and social development, even if he does feel that Blackley has been less than candid with him about department policy.

Social considerations, however, are both a pretext and a context for the play's main preoccupation, which is with how Stone's professional fate illustrates his human character. Thus the play's action takes place—rather statically, for a radio play—in the Stone family home. It is here that Stone has to return now that his public life is in abeyance. The play says, in effect, that the repercussions of public eclipse can best be assessed in private. And it is within the family that Stone's familiar role of "head" meets its ultimate defeat. In D. E. S. Maxwell's words, "Stone's professional anxieties are just one precipitant in a family struggle of wills where authority and judgement are deserting the father. His children bewilder him by giving up their prescribed roles."[10] In other words, Fiona and Walter, the two children in question, cease being children.

These two assert their adulthood by betraying their father. Walter takes the position of head of the detested Clareford school. Fiona, protesting her right to date Sam Daly, son of a long-standing family enemy, eventually goes to London to start a new life with him. In what seems an onset of excessive moralism, the play denies Daniel's children fulfillment. Together they embody their father's professional haplessness and emotional emptiness. Walter may well be, in Fiona's phrase, a "petrified pedagogue,"[11] but his humiliation at the hands of Mr. Blackley seems heavyhanded. Similarly, Fiona is betrayed by Sam Daly's failure to join her in London, and she is obliged to return, shamed, "to this hard house." Already denied Walter's university education—lacking "inclination" according to her father, because "there wasn't any money" according to Fiona (16)—she seems to hold little prospect of anything but the sterility that her father's name connotes.

Yet the play does not end with Daniel perceiving his personal and professional ruin. Instead we find him clinging to the delusion that a third child, Rita, long estranged, is about to return from England to visit him. This delusion is maintained by his loyal wife, Lily, who refuses to tell him that Rita has, in fact, left England for Canada. It is Lily, too, who consoles him with readings from *King Lear*, an allusion the weight of which *To This Hard House* cannot sustain.

As in *A Sort of Freedom*, public and private, blindness and change delimit the concerns of *To This Hard House*. Once again, social issues are not so much considered for their own sakes as they are used as a means of probing the human problems underlying them. Thus, on one level, Daniel Stone is defeated by time and change. But he is also defeated because, deprived of his professional status, he has no inner resources. His lack of heart and spirit are his children's legacy. Were his knowledge of his family's needs nearly as comprehensive as his knowledge of departmental regulations, his final blindness might not have been so complete. Seen from this perspective, Stone's family fortunes are reminiscent of the interconnection between egotism and emotional impoverishment in the makeup of Jack Frazer. Such failings are compounded in Daniel Stone, however, because he ends up as blind to them as Joe Reddin is to *his* limitations. Thus the thematic concerns of *To This Hard House*—public and private, home and work, father and child, authority and responsibility, independence and vulnerability, trust and betrayal—are unified in one character, Daniel Stone, rather than divided between two characters, as in *A Sort of Freedom*.

It seems an exaggeration to say that, "In a technical sense, 'To This Hard House' is even more flawed than 'A Sort of Freedom,'"[12] partly because there seems little to choose between two such obvious 'prentice pieces. The degree to which *To This Hard House* derives from one central character, beside whom all other pale (most notably his wife), is striking and certainly creates imbalances in the play's structure. Giving Stone such prominence may be thought of as an expression in structural terms of the central position he occupied in school and at home. Such prominence, however, tends to weigh down the action of the play by making it too difficult to diversify its effects on the other characters.

Yet the play does introduce a new dimension to Friel's work that will become increasingly important as his drama evolves. The dimension in question is language. While Stone was speaking official, impersonal language with Blackley, he still belonged in the professional world. His trust in the dependability of that language, his pathetic invocations of it in order to shield himself from the truth of his professional situation, suggest the deepseated origins of the blindness that he has collaborated with the world in inflicting upon himself.

A Doubtful Paradise (The Francophile)

Friel's next play represents an attempt at a dramatic departure, having been written for the stage and produced, under the title *The Francophile*, by the Group Theatre, Belfast, in August 1960. Neither play nor production was a success, and Friel recast the material for radio. It was broadcast by the BBC Northern Ireland Home Service in 1962 with the more revealing title *A Doubtful Paradise*.

Set in Derry, the play maps the pretensions of a postal worker in that city and their effects on himself and his family. Willie Logue, the protagonist ("a transmutation of Arthur Miller's Willie Loman [in *Death of a Salesman*]?"),[13] is the francophile in question, though his French is, to put it kindly, limited, as he is the first to admit: "I've been at the language only seven months . . . But in time I hope to study the French classics: Zola, Voltaire, Maritain, Proust, Ibsen, Rosetti . . ."[14] His enthusiasm for French is such that he mistakes a wine salesman for a member of the French nobility, thus precipitating his family into a painful recognition of its emotional inadequacy and its sociocultural disenfranchisement.

Willie's pretensions are not confined to the cultural sphere. He is also under the illusion that every year he will receive the promotion at work he believes he richly deserves. During the course of the play he is once more disappointed. But this social failure acts merely as an understudy of more serious disappointments at the family level. *A Doubtful Paradise*, therefore, is another example of public themes acting more as a framework or support for private concerns, rather than providing a dramatic focus in their own right.

The Logue family consists of wife Maggie (the strongest), son Kevin and daughter Chris (another daughter has already emigrated). The household also contains a lodger, Gerald Sweeney, whose departure halfway through the play, recognized by Willie as a breach in the family, presages larger fissures among the Logues. Gerald has already been instrumental in revealing family failings: Chris, who had planned to go to the movies with Gerald, drops him cold in favor of an evening with Willie and the misperceived Frenchman, M. Tournier. Her flightiness, which her mother Maggie implies Chris shares with her father, has its apotheosis in an elopement with Tournier, which has the same outcome as the Fiona Stone–Sam Daly London episode in *To This Hard House*.

If Chris follows her father's lead in unthinkingly pursuing her need for romance, her brother Kevin resembles Willie by his intellectual orientation. Unlike Chris, Kevin has some awareness of his father's pernicious dreaming, as he reveals in an exchange with Gerald: "That's what happens to everyone who comes into this false atmosphere! He gets ideas! That's what happened to us all! We all get ideas!"(16). In Kevin's case, Willie's ideas have manifested themselves in educating his son for the legal profession, though in the play he has come home to announce his disbarment. At the end of the play, Kevin denounces his father: "Yes, you are an ignorant man. And your ignorance is of the worst sort, the most dangerous sort. Because you are sure and confident in your ignorance"(41). This speech echoes sentiments expressed earlier by Kevin's mother, who reveals that she has prayed for Willie's pride to have a fall. Yet the play declines to let Willie put his feet quite securely on the ground and remove his head from the clouds; it ends with him vowing, "Next winter I'm going to take up . . . Esperanto!"(47).

Though more elaborately worked out than its predecessors, *A Doubtful*

Paradise closely resembles them. Themes such as fathers and children, illusion and reality, society and family obligations are once more to the fore here—so much so, in fact, that it has been seen as "a perceptive attempt to resolve the conflicting purposes of *To This Hard House*."[15] On the other hand, "Willie Logue . . . is . . . worse and more dangerous than Daniel Stone . . . in his dishonesty to himself and the members of his own family."[16] Considered in the light of either character or plot, there seems little to choose between this play and its two forerunners. The inherent drama of the situation is not given a sufficient focus. Willie embodies a conflict he cannot perceive, much less resolve, while those around him perceive the conflict but are just as impotent to resolve it and are inferior, or underdeveloped, embodiments of its general appeal. *A Doubtful Paradise*, therefore, seems "an advance on the radio plays"[17] only when regarded in a charitable light. Perhaps it "reflects Friel's philosophic and artistic stance which is founded on the essential irony of life."[18] But the irony is too broadly conceived and too much a conclusion reached by the audience, rather than a dilemma experienced by the protagonist, to be felt with maximum impact.

Its interest lies more in the way it shows a development in Friel's thought, particularly in the way he is now beginning to perceive the drama latent in language itself. In this sense, *A Doubtful Paradise* develops in significant ways an idea that first appears in *To This Hard House*. The significance of this development emerges in a speech of plaintive rage by Maggie: "I'm sick and tired of words and words and words. That's all I ever hear in this house— word and talk and talk and words. . . . Chris is out there and we're all responsible. You, Willie, for bringing this madness into the house, this madness about culture and learning and all that stuff that was way above and beyond us. You had the wee girl crazed with dreams and images"(31). The subject of *A Doubtful Paradise* suggests itself in Maggie's words. The play depicts Willie's efforts to translate himself out of the disappointments of the workplace and the banality of his surroundings. The means of doing so are to identify with an alternative world, a world synonymous with intellectual attainment and good taste, a world whose capacities to satisfy mind and body provide a model of an integrated existence that is clearly (too clearly, perhaps) the antithesis of Willie's mundane and unproductive existence. *A Doubtful Paradise* is one more Friel work in which illusions carry greater conviction for those who entertain them than does disillusioning society. As the play's closing reference to Esperanto suggests, it is not the practicality of Willie's cultural outlets that is the point, but the assertion of his freedom to choose one. This play may not harness fully the promise of culture as a dramatic theme, or of the duplicitous nature of language, culture's primary medium. But it does show how long such concerns have been on Friel's mind.

The Blind Mice

Friel's next play for radio, *The Blind Mice* was also his second stage play. It was also the first of his works to receive a production outside the North of Ireland: the stage version had a short run at the Eblana Theatre, Dublin, in February 1963. The radio version was broadcast on 28 November 1963 on the BBC Northern Ireland Home Service.

The play tells the story of Father Chris Carroll, who as a Catholic missionary to China was imprisoned in that country, and who now (as the play begins) has been released to a hero's welcome from the world's press and his family back in Ireland. As usual for a Friel play, the action centers less on events than on their effects, which in this case means Father Carroll's casting aside the role of hero and admitting that the only reason for his release was a confession he signed denying his faith. He has no alternative but to make the admission, since news of it has become common knowledge and is brought into the play off the street, as it were—an early, uncharacteristic use by Friel of the public domain. The play takes its departure, therefore, from the contrast between Chris's guilt-ridden sense of his reality and the illusory views of him held by family and society. Ultimately Chris learns to accept himself, but only with the help of a fellow reject and clerical casualty, Father Rooney, a whiskey priest. The more conventional representative of the Church, Father Green, acts merely as an endorser and exploiter of his heroism and, when that is no longer possible, leaves Chris adrift. Similarly, Chris's family has difficulty in accepting him for what he is—which in this case means accepting his human frailty. In particular, his brother John views his brother's failure as an opportunity to vent resentments harbored since childhood and denounces him as "the damned, deceitful Judas" and "that mask of a man."[19] (The latter insult culminates in, "You were never a priest! You were only a consummate actor always!"[49]; a revealing instance of Friel identifying in the language of drama a character who is being cast in the role of outsider.)

Chris is not subjected to the same kind of treatment from the rest of the family, which consists of his mother, Lily; his father, Arthur, a publican; and a sister, Ann. Lily in particular tries to be understanding, while Ann tends to follow John's line (even though her boyfriend, Tom Breslin, is a labor union official and seems somewhat left-wing). Nevertheless, there is no sense of Chris returning in a full sense of the word to the home of which he was once the pride and joy. Given the barrage of reactions with which he has to deal, there is a subtle parallel between his Chinese imprisonment and his presence amidst the family. This parallel is reinforced by the fact that in both cases Chris remains a prisoner of conscience. And the play ends with a rather melodramatic demonstration of Chris, weakened and disturbed by what seems like a heart attack, confusing home and prison by singing the song that kept him sane in China, "Three Blind Mice."

In a number of obvious respects, *The Blind Mice* represents an enlargement of Friel's dramatic scope. Though far from faultless—the cast is too large, the action is static, the claims being made on the protagonist (particularly by Father Green and brother John) are excessive and overstated—*The Blind Mice* is certainly the most substantial of Friel's unpublished plays. It is also the only one of his radio plays to explore, however tentatively, the medium's flexibility by using a wide range of sound effects. Radio drama is also well suited to bringing out the claustrophobia of Chris's moral and physical condition.

Further evidence of this play's more ambitious character is Friel's concentration on the moral, and to some extent the theological, character of the protagonist's situation. Clearly, Chris's desire for innocence (expressed in his admission that when conventional prayers failed to come to him he made "Three Blind Mice" and other nursery rhymes his prayers), his shock at discovering the authentic man beneath the priest's garb, and his desire for forgiveness introduce themes very different from those discussed above. To account for this difference, *The Blind Mice* has been credited with autobiographical origins: "Perhaps at some level it is a transmutation of Friel's own decision of conscience as a novice at Maynooth."[20]

Perhaps. More to the point is this play's successful embodiment of its dramatic tensions *within* a character. The play's familiar oppositions—individual versus family, public versus private, appearance versus reality—are not only part of the scenario's general fabric, they are also reproduced in Chris's inner struggle. The mode of reproduction may be too comprehensive: it seems almost unjust to keep Chris squirming on the moral hook for as long as he does, particularly when, as the end shows, he cannot rescue himself. Nevertheless, the play successfully projects a sense of inner conflict and as such creates not merely a persuasive dramatic situation but an authentic human embodiment of it. In addition, the preoccupation with language seen in *A Doubtful Paradise* is present here again. Here it acts as a subtle characterization of the play's preoccupations, though such a role is by no means negligible, since one version of the play's theme is the question, Under what circumstances can "Three Blind Mice" be a prayer? If Chris Carroll can accept the reality of such circumstances he can accept how human, understandable, and forgivable his responses to them are.

First Success: *The Enemy Within*

Friel's time of apprenticeship as a playwright did not last very long, no doubt because of the experience acquired during his visit in 1963 to Tyrone Guthrie in Minneapolis. The direct result of this visit was the thematically rich and dramaturgically adventurous *Philadelphia, Here I Come!* (1964). As we shall see, however, that play, while making Friel's name, is not as much of an intellectual departure as might be supposed. Even without the decisive trip to Minneapolis, Friel would have sooner rather than later written a play that "dwarfed everything that came before," as has been said of *Philadelphia*.[21]

The justification for such a claim comes from *The Enemy Within* (1962), his first successful and satisfactory work for the stage. In this play Friel takes a number of significant steps forward in technique (the play has a natural rhythm to it), in language (this is the first Friel play in which he doesn't defer to common usage) and in characterization (the play is the first in a series featuring impressively strong protagonists). Thus, while there is no denying the importance of *Philadelphia, Here I Come!* as a landmark in Friel's development, its importance is best appreciated in the context of the early plays, particularly *The Enemy Within*.

Though written after *The Blind Mice*, *The Enemy Within* was produced before it. Its first night was on 6 August 1962 at the Abbey Theatre, Dublin (though at this point in its history the Abbey company was playing at the Queen's Theatre). Thus, Friel's first production outside his native province was a prestigious one.

The play is set in the monastic settlement of St. Columba on the island of Iona off the west coast of Scotland. The time is the seventh century. As Friel himself has said, however, "*The Enemy Within* is neither a history nor a biography but an imaginative account, told in dramatic form, of a short period in St. Columba's thirty-four years of voluntary exile."[22] At the time of the play, Columba's fame for sanctity and missionary zeal has spread far and wide, so much so that a young postulant, Oswald, has travelled from the south of England to partake of it. There is no doubt that Columba is dedicated to his missionary vocation. At the same time, however, he is also claimed by other calls on him, particularly those of home (Columba, besides being a native, and later patron saint, of the city of Derry—as its name in Irish, *Doire*

Columcille, records—is a nobleman of that place and connected by blood to the principal families of the area).

The nature of the more worldly, more political, more emotional claims of home is introduced in the arrival of a messenger, Brian, with word that Columba's presence is required to settle a family feud. Friel's reminder in his preface is pertinent: "When considering these days, one should remember that they were violent and bloody . . . and that it was not until 804, over two hundred years after Columba's death, that monastic communities were formally exempted from military service" (7). Columba feels the enormous strain exerted by the call of his religious duties and that of his family obligations, and the play is built around the tension between these two contending versions of himself. Thus, like *The Blind Mice*, it is a play about conscience and the inner man set in an historical context, rather than being a play about that context.

Columba answers the summons borne by Brian only to find that the situation hardly merited his attention and that, when he returns to Iona at the beginning of act 2, Coarnan the scribe, one of the original twelve who accompanied him into exile, has died without having his wish to die in Ireland fulfilled. Sorrow for not having been present to ease Coarnan's passing and guilt at the waste of energy and ungodly violence that marked his trip spur Columba to exaggerated demonstrations of piety. Yet he is unable to quell his fiery, histrionic temperament, as events at the close of the second act reveal. Naive, ardent Oswald, attempting to explain his own vocational commitment, speaks to Columba as though he has already been canonized. Such an idolatrous approach infuriates Columba, who loses his temper and smacks Oswald across the face, whereupon Oswald runs away and becomes lost, which of course has the effect of reinforcing Columba's sense of his own inadequacy.

Columba's apparent incapacity to deny himself and serve his God comes to a climax in act 3, when he is again summoned to attend to squabbles in the homeland. Matters there seem more serious now, as is indicated by the presence of his brother Eoghan and nephew Aedh in the role of messengers. Yet now, when family loyalty is a more pressing claim than ever, Columba repudiates it, thereby severing not only family ties but also ties with all that his native place means. As though to compensate for this loss, Oswald is found, symbolizing the possibility of integrity and continuity in Columba's self-made, God-fearing world. Structurally, Oswald may be considered the ratifying visitor, in contrast to Columba's landsmen, who are painful distractions from spiritual matters. Oswald can also be thought of as a replacement for Coarnan. The play ends with Columba accepting Oswald as a pretext "to begin again,"[23]—to renew afresh, that is, the struggle with the enemy within.

This play is in virtually every way an improvement on its immediate predecessors in the Friel canon. It successfully establishes a context. Early details about farming and harvesting not only suggest an ongoing community but also establish a theme familiar from the stories, "naturalness." In their unworldliness and simplicity the monks too seem natural, and the tenderness with which Columba treats Coarnan, for example, is—apart from its thematic relevance—a sparkling vignette of the light, playful interaction that is a gloss on the self-sufficing life of the community.

The assurance and tact with which the members of the community treat each other communicates a strong, familial sense of brotherhood. Their freely chosen, mutually beneficial comradeship contrasts with the heavy imposition of obligation on Columba by his family. This contrast is an early example in Friel's work of his redeployment of family structure for dramatic purposes. The artificial family of the monastery conveys a more natural, more life-enhancing sense of purpose and collective trust than anything that Columba's blood relatives convey. Brian, Eoghan, and Aedh bring news only of family feuding, betrayal, and disintegration and as such epitomize the potential for destruction that, according to the predecessors of *The Enemy Within*, families consistently possess.

Columba is the embodiment of Iona's vitalizing spirit. "When he comes on, the atmosphere is breezy and vital" (16), the stage direction reads for Columba's first entry. The energy with which he has sustained Iona and created other missionary outposts on mainland Scotland and beyond is further evidence of how alive Columba is and of what a blessing this ostensibly unalienated life of his seems to be. The blessing is communicated through the obvious love of his companions for him and the natural, unawed manner in which they treat him. Friel is careful to show that, while Columba is head of the community, he does not at all behave in a superior manner, nor is the community organized on rigid, predictable, hierarchical lines.

It is Columba's very vitality, however, that makes his family's claims on him so irresistible. He desires to give to his blood brothers as generously as he gives to his brothers in Christ. Or, rather than self-consciously desiring to do so, he cannot help but self-forgetfully give, irrespective of each given claim's merits. It is his nature to give. Nor is his giving methodical or consistent. His return from Ireland in act 2 has two shared characteristics: Columba recounts the fighting and ancillary family affairs with relish while at the same time distributing gifts to the monks. The stage directions state, "During the distribution of these presents, there is a childlike simplicity and joy in the giving and receiving" (41). The joy and the giving are Columba's hallmarks. He is the first in an illustrious line of outgoing, ebullient, divided Friel protagonists, figures whose appetite for life, whose naturalness, is at once a gift and a cross.

Just as he is loyal to his family, Columba is loyal to Ireland, particularly to the places of his youth. Again, however, this attachment is a source of conflict. As he tells Brian: "I love them . . . and every hill and stream and river and mountain from the top of Fanad down to the waters of blue Melvin. And never a day passes but I see the clouds sit down on Errigal or smell the wrack at Gweebara or hear the wood-pigeons in the oaks of Derry. But I am a priest, a messenger, a man of God, an *alter Christus*—a poor priest, but still a priest. For the sake of Christ, messenger, leave me alone! Don't wedge my frailties between my soul and its Maker!" (30). And after his gift-giving return, having learned of Coarnan's death, Columba beseeches Grillaan, his second in command and spiritual adviser, for help to "Crush this violent Adam into subjection!" (46).

The drama, thus, is an internal one, as it was in *The Blind Mice*, between the "poor priest" and his feeling that "home is a millstone round my neck" (31). External enemies can be dealt with, whether they are Oswald's naiveté or Eoghan's thirst for vengeance. The flaws and aspirations of one's own nature are rather more difficult, if not impossible, to surmount. Divided between worldliness and spirituality, between following his own destiny and obeying the call of traditional family obligation, Columba embodies the inescapably dual character of his own nature, rather than demonstrate a rationalization of its duality. More so than Father Chris Carroll, he takes the weight of his problems upon himself. And whereas Father Carroll reenacted an essentially retrospective perspective of his spiritual crisis, Columba (in keeping with his overall vividness) may be seen actively wrestling with his. His lack of passivity marks an important step forward in Friel's conception of the protagonist and his relationship to ideas of dramatic focus and scene of the action. His lack of passivity makes the play's sense of character problematical. In contrast to, say, Joe Reddin or Daniel Stone, Columba doesn't fit a stereotype. What he experiences as a problem, the audience sees as a revelation, the revelation of a spirit comprehensive enough to contain both pain and faith in equal measure. As to pain, there are Columba's last words on Ireland, the words he uses to dismiss his brother Eoghan and all he stands for: "Go back to those damned mountains and seductive hills that have robbed me of my Christ! You soaked my sweat! You sucked my blood! You stole my manhood, my best years! What more do you demand of me, damned Ireland? My soul? My immortal soul? Damned, damned, damned Ireland!—(*His voice breaks.*) Soft, green Ireland—beautiful, green Ireland—my lovely green Ireland"

(70). For faith, there are the words of rededication that greet Oswald's return and with which the play ends.

In keeping with enriched themes and more complex protagonists, other aspects of the play, such as its language and its structure, show considerable advances over even its companion piece, *The Blind Mice*. Obviously, finding a language that will not distract by quaintness or affectation from the play's dramatic issues must be a concern of any author dealing with historically remote material. Friel, in his preface, acknowledges that "I put modern prose into the mouths of the characters" (7). Yet the language is far from prosaic; it has a ring and a resonance to it that fully conveys both Columba's vitality and that of the dramatic issues.

The play's verbal richness may be seen in its use of anecdote, memory, and allusion to diversify characters and their world. Such usages offer a fresh angle on Columba's dilemma by presenting him as a character who fears that the memories of his past may jeopardize his future. In addition, the playwright's ear for echoes and correspondences is displayed to good effect when Eoghan tries to enlist Columba by calling the trouble at home "a religious matter" (65). Or again, when Eoghan leaves and Columba declares himself to be spiritually "empty," Oswald enters, saying he came back "because I was hungry" (71). By such relatively deft touches, the play's language underwrites a sense of the indissolubility of Columba's inner conflict and, together with what D. E. S. Maxwell has called the "mosaic of accents"[24] which the characters' speech comprises, makes up the greater linguistic freedom and variety of *The Enemy Within*.

Structurally speaking, the play has a conventional three-act format, with the second act divided into two scenes. The play's development is conceived in chronological terms, though this is not its only principle of development. Cutting against the grain of chronological evolution is a sense of repetition and intensification. At the end of the play, Columba is more or less as we found him at the beginning, with the same unresolved conflict and the same spirited involvement with it. As Maxwell has noted, "The end of the play is a beginning."[25] The play has been criticized because "the two scenes of Columba's temptations from home and family may be too synchronized."[26] This point overlooks the greater call exerted by the reasons for the second "temptation," which makes Columba's rejection all the more difficult, thus intensifying what is in some respects the play's climactic, or at any rate most obviously dramatic, scene. The interleaving of ends and beginnings allows the play to suggest a more complex rhythm to life than that admitted by Columba's view of himself as either a priest and nothing else or a family exile and nothing else. The existence of that rhythm is what Grillaan identifies in

Columba's name: "In some men . . . sanctity is a progression, a building of stone upon stone, year after year, until the edifice is complete. In other men, it is in the will and determination to start, and then to start again, and then to start again, so that their life is a series of beginnings. You are of the second kind, Columba" (47). It is in the honoring of that cycle that the play's theme and structure achieve their most impressive degree of articulateness. And in finding opportunity for renewal in endings, this play marks a distinctive departure from the author's earlier dramatic efforts.

Not surprisingly, *The Enemy Within* has been seen as Friel's first satisfactory play. The author himself has given this view a tepid endorsement: "It's not good, but it was a commendable sort of play. There's nothing very wrong with it and there's certainly nothing very good about it."[27] The "consistently favourable"[28] reception the first production received is echoed, by and large, by both Maxwell and Dantanus, who in addition emphasize its significance as a launching pad for Friel's career in the theater.[29]

Philadelphia, Here I Come!

Friel's greatest hit was first produced at the Gaiety Theatre, Dublin, on 28 September 1964 and subsequently at the Helen Hayes Theater, New York, where beginning on 16 February 1966 it had a run of nine months; and the Lyric Theatre, in London's West End, where it opened on 21 September 1967. It has remained one of Friel's best-known and best-loved plays, has frequently been revived (most notably, perhaps, in an Abbey Theatre production in 1982), and represents the definitive breakthrough in his career, not only in terms of fame but also in terms of technique and theme.

The play is the first of Friel's to be set in the village of Ballybeg, though, as before, it is less the world in general that provides the setting as a family within that world. The family in question is the O'Donnells, consisting of S. B., a merchant, county councillor, and general pillar of the community; his son Gar; and a servant Madge (Mrs. O'Donnell is dead). Gar is the protagonist. The action takes place during his last night at home—he is off to Philadelphia in the morning—and largely consists of memories of Gar's past and projections of his future. Gar's incessant mental activity is interrupted by visits from friends and other members of the community, including Kate Doogan (now Mrs. King), the girl he did not have the nerve to marry.

Despite the presence of these visitors and the innovative (for Friel) use of flashback, the action is once again, as in *The Enemy Within* and *The Blind Mice*, conceived of as the articulation of the personality, rather than in terms of a dynamic, developmental interaction between an individual and his world. The conception works particularly well in this case, however, since the lack of physical activity as such draws attention to the limbo of waiting Gar has to endure before his new life can begin.

This state is explored to great effect and is the source of the play's most adventurous innovation, the portrayal of Gar by two actors, one playing Public Gar and the other Private Gar. Waiting to leave, negotiating the peculiarly suspended sense of himself evoked by the line "it's all over . . . And it's all about to begin,"[30] Gar is prey to indeterminacy, to the finality of choosing, to irreconcilable ambivalences. The line just quoted echoes analogous sentiments in *The Enemy Within*, and *Philadelphia*, with its themes of exile and family, community and selfhood, vulnerability and commitment, is that play's natural successor.

To underline the fact that the play's subject is not exile as such, or Ballybeg as such, but the implications of choosing one or the other, it ends not by showing Gar making a final commitment but with him saying "I don't know. I-I-I don't know" (110). The play's ending offers an epiphanous crystallization of the condition it has been depicting. It is in the "sort of freedom" conferred by having to choose between two socially and culturally defined positions that Friel has found his theme, enabling *Philadelphia, Here I Come!* to be seen as one of the pivotal points in his playwriting career.

In addition, the ending draws attention to the play's relative lack of interest in narrative, or in events unfolding in a consistent manner toward a denoument. As D. E. S. Maxwell has noted: "The logic of the play is not in plot contrivance or 'what-happens-next,' but in its delicate montage of past and present experience and feeling."[31] This suppression of narrative and its teleology facilitates the complex and indeterminate use of time in the play, a use that in turn accommodates the conflicting presences of memory and desire in Gar's makeup. Thus the perception of *Philadelphia* as a career breakthrough, while rightly emphasizing the play's thematic and dramaturgical sophistication, should not overlook the play's subtle intellectual underpinnings.

The intellectual interest of *Philadelphia* is heavily disguised by the interest of its theme and the novelty of its stagecraft. Thematically speaking, it is possible to be misled by the geographical promise of the play's title. Philadelphia may be regarded as a name for the exile from family and from Ballybeg which Gar has long felt. Travel to the United States will clearly be a physical demonstration of this condition, but it will not necessarily cure it, particularly since Gar's social status and job prospects will hardly be improved by his new life. He will still be attached to his family, in the person of his aunt Lizzy, who is as erratic and garrulous as Gar's father is predictable and taciturn. And instead of laboring in his father's store, he will be a clerk in a Philadelphia hotel. America, therefore, may prove to be a reprise rather than a revolution.

To Gar, Ballybeg has meant lovelessness, boredom, and the fecklessness of imperfectly realized ambitions. As his Ballybeg life presses in on him for the last time, its emptiness and stultification become evident. Gar's loutish friends, the unctiously banal clichés of the parish priest, the demoralized state of Gar's old schoolteacher, and above all Gar's nonrelationship with his father bespeak an emotional and cultural wasteland. The one bright spot for Gar has been Kate Doogan, with whom he was in love and (refreshingly, for an Irish play) in lust. But a combination of economic insecurity, diffidence in the presence of Kate's father, Senator Doogan, and her family's assumption that Kate will marry within her class—in other words, a coalition of personal impoverishment and social expectations—defeats Gar.

When to his surprise Kate comes to say goodbye, Gar ends her visit with a denial of friendship's tenderness and for his coup de grace uses the words of an earlier visitor, the dilapidated old schoolmaster, Boyle: "Impermanence—anonymity—that's what I'm looking for; a vast restless place that doesn't give a damn about the past" (81). The sentiment is as little Gar's as the words are; indeed, Boyle himself doesn't believe them, as is borne out by the fact that his advice to "forget Ballybeg and Ireland" is followed immediately by "Perhaps you'll write me" (47)—a request for remembrance. In any case, Gar's problem is that he is unable to obliterate Ballybeg and the human experiences that typify it. He cannot find within himself an indifference to match its apparent indifference to him: instead he finds rage, disgust, and pain. Gar spends more time looking back than he does looking forward. Private Gar remarks: "You know what you're doing, don't you, laddybuck? Collecting memories and images and impressions that are going to make you bloody miserable; and in a way that's what you want, isn't it?" (54).

The source of Gar's pain and rage is emotional, as his cruelly outspoken response to Kate's visit suggests. In fact, Kate seems to be the immediate reason for Gar's emigration. For, as the play's most substantial flashback reveals, it is on Kate's wedding day that his childless aunt Lizzy from Philadelphia comes visiting with her husband Con and friend Ben. Lizzy, made emotionally susceptible by the sight of childhood places, by the sight of her dead sister's only child, and by the awareness of her own childlessness, recruits Gar to fill her American life. Gar, made emotionally vulnerable by the wedding, makes a "silly and impetuous" (65) acceptance of her offer; as he ruefully reflects, "She got you soft on account of the day it was" (65).

Central as Kate is to the development of the situation, Gar's experience of her underscores emotional pain at a deeper level of his makeup. This level is occupied by his relationship with his father, a relationship that ushers in and closes out the action of the play. S. B., which to Gar stands for "Screwballs," is an undemonstrative, unappealing, unprepossessing figure, his mind fixed on practical matters and his emotions heavily under wraps. His self-possession and inexpressiveness stand in explicit and frustrating contrast to his son's in-security and histrionics. Indeed, perhaps the playwright may have painted too unambiguous a portrait of S. B. for the audience to accept that he married Gar's mother, or to believe what the servant Madge says about him. Yet, quite unexpectedly, at the end of the play he does reveal, though not to Gar, that he too has memories of his son and feelings resulting from them. This twist in his character is a good example of Friel's use of a strategy of unpre-dictability in presenting his material. (Another example is that of Ned, the most loutish of Gar's peers, taking off his belt and giving it to Gar as a part-ing gift. And of course, Gar, split between public and private versions of him-self, neither of which he can adequately control, is virtually a definition of unpredictability.) In addition, however, S. B.'s memory and the fact that it is accompanied both by emotion and by an incapacity to put that emotion to some use in his relationship with Gar show that he too is caught. He is able neither to deny the emotion nor to admit it. Gar is not his victim; he is his heir. He represents an intensification of his father's mentality rather than the antithesis of it.

Gar and his father possess a mutuality at a textual level that they decline to control or acknowledge at a personal level. The repressive character of their relationship is both a deficiency and a reality. Such a degree of interaction be-tween levels shows how adeptly Friel allows his characters the subjective free-dom of their temperaments through his firm control of the integrative, objectivizing requirements of the text. As ever, Friel's subject is human na-ture, its vagaries and imperfections. What he has succeeded in addressing in *Philadelphia, Here I Come!*, however, is not the regrettable existence of flaws and deficiencies but the expressive potential they contain.

This thematic adjustment is given its most complete expression in the character of Gar. The fact of his being divided reemphasizes the paradoxi-cally enabling nature of incompleteness, which is further underlined by the strict injunctions in the play's introductory material:

The two Gars, Public Gar and Private Gar, are two views of the one man. Public Gar is the Gar that people see, talk to, talk about. Private Gar is the unseen man, the man within, the conscience, the alter ego, the secret thoughts, the id.

Private Gar, the spirit, is invisible to everybody, always. Nobody except Public Gar hears him talk. But even Public Gar, although he talks to Private Gar occasionally, never sees him and *never looks at him* [emphasis in the original]. One cannot look at one's alter ego. (11–12)

Private Gar is the one who has no place in Ballybeg: he is the Gar who is in exile. He also is the witty, outrageous, satirical, sensitive, fantasizing, distancing Gar. He is the essentially theatrical Gar, who acts out what his public brother has no audience for. He is the Gar who utters what Ballybeg unthinkingly, unfeelingly, unconsciously perhaps, consigns to silence. He is the Gar who compels Public Gar "in whispered shout" to say, "Screwballs, say something! Say something, father!" (83), though at the time both Gars are alone and desolate after Kate Doogan's farewell visit.

Private Gar, therefore, is by far the abler and freer of the two, yet he is also the one whose independent existence can be upheld only by a willing suspension of disbelief. He is Gar's potential, rather than Gar's reality. He is also what the culture of Ballybeg has no room for. The division of Gar, thus, is an imaginative measure intended as a critique of local and familial narrowness and repetitious, mundane routine. The two Gars, taken jointly, comprise a picture of wholeness that their environment will not allow. Or, since it is impossible to take the two Gars as one, the environment constitutes a reality that Private Gar cannot alter. The obvious element of contrivance in Friel's strategy is what the revelation of a flawed reality crucially depends upon.

Distance, then, in various conceptions of the term, is at the center of *Philadelphia, Here I Come!* It is given geographical, cultural, and social expression in the play's title, psychological expression in the two Gars, and emotional expression in Public Gar's two stunted relationships (with Kate and his father). The play's ultimate and most telling expression of distance, however, is silence. When words fail Gar, emotional disenfranchisement is the inevitable result. His experiences with Kate's father and with S. B. say as much. Yet, as Private Gar's verbosity indicates, it is only through words that some degree of integration may be possible between Public Gar and his needs. And it is the silence of others, notably S. B., that fuels Private Gar's verbosity. The play cannot help but criticize the distance that it shows silence enjoining. Thus, *Philadelphia, Here I Come!* validates its own medium—a medium that requires that certain indispensable statements be made. In doing so, it validates the presence of its most theatrical, most artificial, and most artful character, Private Gar. For these reasons, in addition to those that show the play to be the fruitful outcome of Friel's theatrical apprenticeship, *Philadelphia, Here I Come!* may be instructively regarded not only as, in its own right, one of the author's most memorable works, but as a play that, as we shall see, embodies in clear and original form many of his career's artistic and cultural preoccupations. Here is the first decisive formation of that matrix of themes—conflict between public and private selves, solitariness, lovelessness, family tensions, cultural aspiration and cultural impoverishment—that has continued to nourish Friel's dramatic imagination. As for *Philadelphia* itself, it is difficult not to conclude that, in the words of Robert Hogan, "in sum, this is a brilliant and beautiful study of isolation and its inevitably accompanying anguish. Well played, it should leave its audience both charmed and bruised."[32] Critical responses of the play have generously endorsed these terms of appreciation.

Chapter Three
On with the Show

The commentator who noted of Private Gar in *Philadelphia* that "it is his voice that carries the mockery of the narrow routine of village life, and of the daily repetition of the same patterns of speech and behaviour"[1] might well have credited the play itself with performing the same function for contemporary Irish theater. Private Gar's articulateness draws attention by its bracing freshness to the play's novel rethinking of character, place, and time, so that *Philadelphia, Here I Come!* as a whole speaks in the tone of a theatrical tradition (that of the Irish kitchen drama) in the process of renewing itself.

It would appear that Friel himself is of the same opinion, in view of his attitude to *Philadelphia's* predecessors: "The first play I did was a play called *This Doubtful Paradise.* . . . It was a very bad play and I like to forget about it. Then I did *The Blind Mice,* which was also a bad play and which I have now [1965] withdrawn. The next one was *The Enemy Within,* which was a solid play. . . . It's not good, but it was a commendable sort of a play. I wouldn't put it any stronger than that. There's nothing very wrong with it and there's certainly nothing very good about it. It's a solid play."[2] Certainly, as D. E. S. Maxwell has written, *Philadelphia* is a play "of a totally different order of achievement from its predecessors."[3]

But the difference is not merely discernible in Maxwell's view that *Philadelphia* "is a statement about Ireland, the Ireland of religious and sexual frigidity, of overbearing old age, of joyless, close-mouthed rural puritanism; and of their opposites."[4] The difference lies in the immeasurably greater degree of dramaturgical sophistication Friel brings to such material, treating it with a freedom that the Gars, trapped in the reality of the play's culture, can only dream about. And it is to this newfound artistic freedom that Friel now devotes his creative energies—in the musical conception of *The Loves of Cass McGuire,* in the diptych *Lovers,* in the structure of episodes, conventional acts, and scenes used in *Philadelphia* and developed in *Crystal and Fox.*

Friel has come in for a certain amount of criticism for his dramaturgical innovations, what one critic has called "neo-Expressionistic crutches and neo-Brechtian gimmicks."[5] The innovations, however, are neither self-serving nor merely modish. Their significance derives from the playwright's belief that the days of the solid, well-made play are gone, the play with a beginning, a middle and an end, where in Act I a dozen carefully balanced characters are thrown into an arena and are presented with a problem, where in Act II they attack the problem and one another according to the Queensberry Rules of Drama, and in Act III the problem is cosily resolved and all concerned are a lot wiser, a little nobler, and preferably a bit sadder. And these plays are finished because we know that life is about as remote from a presentation-problem-resolution cycle as it can be.[6]

Friel does not criticize the theatrical complacency of the well-made play on the grounds of its thematic insufficiency. The point is not what plays are about but how they are about it. Thematic continuity is a crucial feature of Friel's plays—D. E. S. Maxwell, for example, believes that *The Enemy Within* initiates "a kind of tetralogy on the theme of love and family."[7] The strength and significance of this thematic continuity is highlighted by the challenges of unfamiliar technique. It is the originality of Friel's approach to "the theme of love and family," not the originality of that theme in itself, that matters here. Such an emphasis underlines Friel's efforts to evolve a dramaturgy that would clarify his preoccupation with various forms of division and connection—interpersonal, temporal, intrapersonal—so comprehensively inaugurated by *Philadelphia, Here I Come!* Friel is reportedly "suspicious of a theme or subject that does not generate its own answer to the question of form."[8] His most successful plays confirm the value and validity of such aesthetic sensitivity.

Friel's Theater of Character

From the outset, Friel's has been a theater of character. His main concern is with a central human figure or type—the man of vision (Columba), the youth (Gar), the man of principle in the earlier plays—and with those elements of individual experience that question the moral cost of maintaining the integrity of the type. The most significant tension in Friel's early drama is not between self and world but between the unpredictable freedom of the self, considered in individual terms, and the rather repressive security of the self, considered in generic terms. And one of the sources of the drama in *The Enemy Within* and *Philadelphia* is the conflict between the varieties of selves that the protagonists contain and are obliged to acknowledge.

Columba is a man of God, an exile, a family member, a man of action, an exemplar, a fraternal comrade . . . The list could be extended. For Columba, the challenge is to give due attention to each of these roles, each one of which to some degree impinges on, and even compromises, the others. Not surpris-

ingly, therefore, he seeks to reconcile them in one tenable, admirable designa-
tion, that of saintliness. Columba's human reality, however, consists of the
unnerving and unpredictable flux of role-playing that he is called upon to do.
The unformed, unstable, restless spirit that animates him is his reality, not
the narrow cell of stereotype.

Gar O'Donnell also plays a variety of roles. And as in Columba's case,
these are not confined to roles chosen for him by the playwright; or rather, the
playwright invites the audience to collaborate in the naturalistic convention
that Gar's roles are a function of nature rather than of art. Thus, he is a son, a
friend, an ex-lover, an imaginative young man. As in *The Enemy Within,* but
rather more pointedly, there seems to be an antagonism between these various roles in which nature has cast Gar; and this antagonism is highlighted
and aggravated by the self-conscious, or artful, or individuating roles in
which he casts himself. Once again, the competition between the various
human options available to, or embodied by, Gar is what appoints him to his
central presence in the drama. The drama's success—its projection of a
human image—is directly related to its protagonist's failure to master the
flux of reality.

Retaining this conception of character, based on contradictoriness, impulse, variety, and unpredictability, Friel now goes on to develop a mode of
theatrical presentation which will do justice to it. Thus, in *The Loves of Cass
McGuire,* the eponymous protagonist dominates the proceedings to an even
greater degree than did Gar and Columba. The reason for her doing so is that
Friel has decided to reveal her life story in terms of its erratic flux. In this play
not only is the focus on a particularly critical, terminal moment in the phase
of the protagonist's life, but this focus is used to dramatize this moment's
place in the pattern of Cass's existence. By the use of flashback and chronological disorientation Cass is shown to be an embodiment of flux and of the
fight against it. In *Lovers,* which consists of two plays, *Winners* and *Losers,*
the winners are two young lovers whose early deaths protect them from the
struggle that divides Cass McGuire. Andy Tracey, the protagonist of *Losers,*
is a loser because he exists in conditions that do not admit change, but rather
consist of a ritualized, claustrophobic round of sameness. The eternal present
in which the couple in *Winners* are imaginatively preserved—that glorious
day, when there seems to be so much time that time seems an irrelevant dimension—has a freedom and openness that the play's static staging effectively underlines. In contrast, the fluent dissolves in *Losers* between past and
present, indoor and outdoor, mock, in dramaturgical terms, the protagonist's
entrapment. Finally, in *Crystal and Fox,* which consolidates Friel's work in
the theater-of-character phase of his career, Fox Melarkey applies his moral

energies to reducing the fluctuating restlessness of his life by slowly eliminating the number of roles for which he considers himself responsible. He wants to equate the condition resulting from this purge with innocence, regardless of the damage that it inevitably entails. Dramaturgically, this play acts as an increasingly bleak series of "episodes" (as Friel calls them) in unmasking. The play devours itself: when there are no more masks for Fox to wear, the play ends. Without illusion there can be no theater; without uncertainty there can be no reality. The interrelationship between these two preconditions forms the basis for growth and development of Friel's Theater of character.

The Loves of Cass McGuire

The immediate successor of *Philadelphia, Here I Come!*, *The Loves of Cass McGuire* had its first performance at New York's Helen Hayes Theater on October 6, 1966, with Ruth Gordon in the title role.

It has been called *Philadelphia's* "sister play,"[9] and in terms of its story line it certainly seems to be the earlier play's counterpart. Instead of featuring a timid young provincial on the eve of immigration, *The Loves of Cass McGuire* depicts a brazen, aging heroine who has just returned from having spent most of her life in New York City. The home to which Cass returns is as emotionally sterile as that which Gar O'Donnell is about to leave, so much so that her family installs her in Eden House, a less than paradisal old persons' home.

As in *Philadelphia, Here I Come!*, the starkness of the story line is relieved by the protagonist's capacity to dream, though Cass is less inclined to do so than Gar and earlier members of the Friel dramatic family. Her reluctance is more than compensated for, however, by all of the other characters, in particular two of Cass's fellow exiles in "Eden," Trilbe Costello and Mr. Ingram. Though this couple are by far the play's most compulsive fantasists, their capacity for delusion, dream, and self-deception is shared by each of Cass's families, her blood relatives and her companions in Eden House. Thus in thematic terms the world with which Cass has to deal possesses a unity, but no member of that world is able to experience that unity, certainly not with any degree of consistency. Cass comes closest; thus her eventual failure hits home with an appropriate climactic resonance.

Cass is a wonderful character, the first in a notable line of Friel women, and conveys in her own terms the same sense of vitality that makes Columba and Gar such attractive stage presences—the audience's first sight of her is as "she charges on stage."[10] Forced to emigrate while in her teens because of sexual exuberance, she returns with her natural swagger and extroversion still ostensibly to the fore, accentuated as well as tarnished by her fifty-two years as a waitress in "this joint on the lower East Side" (17). But because she is "a gust of vulgar skepticism,"[11] offensive alike to her brother Harry and his family and to the other residents of Eden House, Cass's return proves not to be the escape she seeks, or rather, it is not an escape on her own terms.

Since she is no more than a nominal member of her family, and since she has no cultural attachments to the play's unspecified locale, Cass is given no choice but to fall back on her own psychic resources. Her private self is required to be the inspiration for her pubic behavior. This is a state of affairs that Cass does her utmost to resist, and because of this resistance she possesses a reality that the rest of the people in the play have, in different ways, forgone.

In Cass's case, private self is a synonym for memory—as it is for Gar O'Donnell and Columba. Yet, for as long as she is able, Cass attempts to survive intact in the terms she asserts in an early exchange with brother Harry:

> HARRY: You may think you can seal off your mind like this, but you can't. The past will keep coming back to you.
>
> CASS: I live in the present, Harry boy! Right here and now! (16)

But there is so little in the present to live for that Harry's warning comes all too true. When Cass finds this to be the case, she can neither resist the force of memory nor rationalize away its pain. She is unable to lie to herself about her memories: she has to play them straight. The memories are of loves betrayed—of her father deserting the family, of her unsavory and unsuitable New York roommate Jeff, of the family's implicit rejection of the ten dollars a week Cass sent home in order to help them (in order, that is, to remain influentially involved with their lives). As Harry explains, "we never really needed it. And now it's all intact. . . . And it makes you independent of everyone" (72). But it is precisely such feelings of isolation, redundancy, and lovelessness that Cass resists, as she must, being incapable of seeing her desire to give continually considered unnecessary by her prospective recipients.

The reality of Cass's struggle with herself is reinforced when contrasted with the pervasive sense of cover-up and self-deception exemplified by the other characters. Harry's family is rather less unified than Cass has been led to believe. But no sooner has he admitted this and invited Cass home to share Christmas with him (conferring on her the well-meaning though insulting status of a child-substitute) than his wife Alice, "on the point of tears," insists: "The children are all coming . . ." (111).

Much more crucial to an appreciation of Cass's position, however, is the Eden House couple, Trilbe and Ingram, the rhapsodists, each of whom, in the words of Friel's note at the beginning of the play, "takes the shabby and unpromising threads of his past life and weaves them into a hymn of joy, a gay and rapturous and exaggerated celebration of a beauty that might have been." This odd couple live in a totally private world, which they articulate in musical language. The substance of their long speeches consists of a fantasy emotional life, a far cry from the unfulfilled loves of Cass McGuire. Friel goes on to say that these speeches, or "rhapsodies," may be accompanied by the *Liebestod* from Wagner's *Tristan und Isolde*. The story of these lovers is referred to in the course of the rhapsodies. Friel is also thinking in terms of Wagner's technical innovations of leitmotiv and "endless melody."

Cass's first experience of rhapsody elicits indifference and implicit incredulity.

TRILBE: Join with us . . . for we have the truth.

CASS: Sure . . . sure . . . (44)

Trilbe's truth, as she says, consists of "the past, and all the riches I have, and all that nourishes me" (45). Such truth, obviously, is imaginative, the counterpart to the harsh realities with which Cass is trying to contend. And as for the rhapsodies, D. E. S. Maxwell rightly points out: "Their intention is not to represent literally any real form of neurotic behaviour. They are stylized expression, dramatic allegories, of a psychological state that compensates for painful fact in the refuge of a private world."[12] The rhapsodies are strategies of escape and abstraction from lovelessness. Cass, on the other hand, intends to control rather than escape; the play is an enactment of the fate of this intention.

Just as the rhapsodies are both thematic and technical developments (or thematic developments cast as technical developments), so too Cass's feisty desire to control is given technical expression. One of the reasons she pays little attention to Trilbe at first is that she is too busy addressing the audience (to whose existence Trilbe is oblivious). Such addresses are a cogent expression both of Cass's need to make meaningful human contact and of the lack of reciprocity with which her efforts are met. And by attempting to break the theatrical illusion, the addresses are consistent with Cass's generally iconoclastic temperament. The illusion remains unbroken, however: the audience does not respond, does not know how to respond. Thus, Cass's attempt to break out of her condition only has the result of confirming her in it.

Cass tries in other ways to seize control of the play's form. Harry, as conventionally minded and manipulative here as elsewhere, determines that "it must be shown slowly and in sequence why you went to Eden House" (14).

Cass's attitude to this approach is to demand that "the story begins where I say it begins, and I say it begins with me stuck in the gawddam workhouse!" (13). But as with many other elements in her condition, she is too late. The forms her presence is required to occupy have already been determined. And as though to confirm this, Cass's acceptance of Eden House and a world of illusion comes immediately after "Cass goes downstage and searches for the audience again. Finds no one" (116). Instead:

> TRILBE: Never mind . . . you have us. Our world is real, too.
>
> INGRAM: Our world is just as real. (116)

D.E.S. Maxwell's analysis of the play's technical aspects is worth quoting: "There is an absorbing dramatic tension between the play's apparent promise of social comedy, and the gradual dissolution of Cass's will, where the real conflict is taking place. The transactions with the audience evolve into a dynamic emblem of the diminishing contact that Cass is striving to preserve. . . . The fluidity of time and setting, equally functional, corresponds to Cass's own vacillations, as past and present threaten to coalesce into dream."[13]

There is an irresistible sense of defeat when Cass opts for the world of rhapsody, when the more vital sense of home is conveyed in her statement, "That's what it's all about, isn't it—coming home?" (78) and the close of the play, when she "brightens, looks around the common room with calm satisfaction," and says, "Home at last. Gee, but it's a good thing to be home" (139).

Illusion may be a saving grace. The imagination may be the ultimate form of resistance. But the models of illusion and imaginativeness are so bloodless and sexless, in comparison to Cass, that it is difficult not to think of her survival on the terms available as a defeat. These terms are formal, structured, and all-embracing; Cass, on the other hand, is informal, chaotic, and strongly individualized. But there is no room for the manifest energy that derives from those elements of Cass's makeup. Her story is one of resisting stereotypes, as the play deftly insinuates by making her seem like a raucous, drunken stage-Irishwoman and then obliging the audience to admit that there is a lot more to her than that. She becomes, however, absorbed into what Friel, in his prefatory note calls "the ritual of the action." Cass, too, becomes a rhapsodist: "And we moved into this great big ten-roomed apartment on the West Side, and from our bedroom window we could see the ships sailing off to South America . . . and Ireland . . . And all round the walls were pictures of Harry's kids . . . and regular as the clock came their letters . . . And when I came back home they were all down at Cork to meet me . . ." (129).

Like her immediate predecessors among Friel protagonists, Cass McGuire is a divided character who suffers the heartache and the pangs of consciousness that division entails. Once again a public, ebullient self is contrasted to a private, lonely self. Once again family relations render feelings inarticulate, the only response to which is the discovery of alternative emotional language. Once again the protagonist is found, for the most part, in an indeterminate state, experiencing conflicting demands on the inner self. Cass's revelation of her ultimate fate ("the gawddam workhouse") so early in the play is a reminder of other statements in *Philadelphia, Here I Come!* and *The Enemy Within* about beginnings and endings entailing each other, and emphasizes Cass's state of indeterminacy. (The criticism that *The Loves of Cass McGuire* is lacking in plot[14] seems beside the point.)

It is possible that *The Loves of Cass McGuire* is an overcrowded play. The presence of Cass's mother and of her nephew Don does not seem strictly necessary. The decision to make Cass the sole source of reminiscence, rather than use flashbacks in which the persons being recalled appear, as they do in *Philadelphia, Here I Come!*, may be an indication of how concerned Friel was not to repeat a technique. No doubt the weight of reminiscing which Cass is asked to carry, and her struggle with it, keep her isolation and subjectivity strictly in focus. But perhaps her history could be rendered more graphically with the use of flashback. Also, the Christmas backdrop to Cass's installation in Eden House does not seem strictly necessary: the play already contains plenty of evidence of family coldheartedness. But while *The Loves of Cass McGuire* may suffer from a degree of overelaboration, it shows Friel consolidating his thematic grasp by diversifying his technical range. The play may be considered, as Friel says in his prefatory note, "a concerto in which Cass McGuire is the soloist." The score from which she performs, however, retains a problematic and moving conception of harmony.

Lovers

Friel's next piece for the theater, *Lovers,* consists of two short plays, *Winners* and *Losers,* featuring different characters in explicitly contrasting situations. It was first produced at the Gate Theatre, Dublin, on 18 July 1967. The text of the play is dedicated to Tyrone Guthrie.[15]

Of the two plays, *Winners* is the more arresting. As in the case of its counterpart, the title is ironic. Joe and Mag, the two youngsters who spend the day surveying with playful verve the life around them and the life they are about to begin together, never get any further with that life: the play ends with them unknowingly on their way to being drowned. The implication of the title is that they are the lucky ones. In contrast, Andy in *Losers* after many years secures Hannah, his heart's delight, in marriage. As a result, however, he is obliged to live out an unnaturally constrained existence.

There is more to both plays than plot. Both works, in their way, are exposés of small-town mores. In *Winners* Mag is pregnant and she and Joe are to be married as soon as they have completed their school examinations. In *Losers* piety is carried to a positively destructive degree. Moreover, in both plays Friel continues to pursue dramaturgical innovation.

The most successful element of *Winners* is the exuberance and intensity of the young couple. Mag Enright is "bubbling with life,"[16] while Joe Brennan "is at the age when he is earnest about life; and he has a total and touching belief in the value and importance of education" (5–6). Their dispositions are all the more refreshing in view of the obviously uphill struggle that awaits them as a married couple, an emblem of which is the room overlooking the local abbatoir which is all they can get in the way of a home for themselves. They are touchingly devoted to the conception of their own unity in a world full of discouraging fissures.

Some of the world's divisiveness is the result of social attitudes fostered by the Church (both youngsters are Catholics). And for all their closeness, Joe and Mag are vulnerable to class divisions. Joe, retaliating for a careless allusion to his parents' lack of education, berates Mag: "Well, let me tell you, madam, that my father may be temporarily unemployed, but he pays his bills; and *my* mother may be a charwoman but she isn't running out to the mental hospital for treatment every couple of months. And if you think the Brennans aren't swanky enough for you, then by God you shouldn't be in such a hurry to marry one of them!" (71–72). Other divisions, however, have more imponderable origins and seem to be in the nature of things, a nature Joe and Mag deny because they are young, in love, inexperienced, and untried. In particular, judging by the accounts each of them give of their parents' marriages, personal relationships seem peculiarly imperfect. The world may be full of unpromising precedents, but Joe and Mag implicitly believe themselves to have the energy to escape their influence.

One reason to infer this belief is their obvious emotional honesty. Their feelings toward each other are expressed fully, openly, without reservation, and often with painfully naive sincerity. As a counterpart to their lack of gamesmanship between themselves, they are very much given to parodying the adult world and its authority figures. Both Joe and Mag have a flair for mimicry and mime, by which theatrical means they believe those more powerful than themselves can be kept at bay. The play allows the twosome to give full play to their subjective feelings. These feelings gain strength, variety, and unpredictability here from the characters, once again, being in an indeterminate, transitional state:

> MAG: I'm a woman at seventeen, and I wouldn't be a schoolgirl again, not for all the world.
>
> JOE: I suppose I'm a man, too. (82)

And on her way to the lake in which she will drown:

> *Maggie suddenly leaps to her feet. Her face is animated, her movements quick and vital, her voice ringing.*
>
> MAG: The past's over! And I hate this waiting time! I want the future to happen—I want to be in it—I want to be in it with you! (84–85)

Little does she know that this joyful anticipation of the life to come is to have an outcome she cannot possibly foresee.

The audience, however, not only can foresee it but knows it to be an accomplished fact. The information is provided by the play's other two characters, named Man and Woman, of whose existence Joe and Mag are blissfully and necessarily unaware. Their presence places the two youngsters' vitality, individuality, and subjectivity within a framework of generalized objectivity. They are the voices of fact, of documentary record, of impassive commentary: "They are the Commentators. . . . Each has a book on his knee—not a volume, preferably a bound manuscript—and they read from this every so often. Their reading is impersonal, completely without emotion: their function is to give information. At no time must they reveal an attitude to their material" (5).

Shortly after the commentators convey incontrovertible evidence of the drowning (the bodies are discovered more than a fortnight after Joe and Mag disappear), Mag quotes *King Lear* from one of her schoolbooks: "As flies to wanton boys are we to the gods; they kill us for their sport" (40). The Commentators have the effect of reinforcing this terrifying summation of human existence, though without actively conniving at the sport.[17] The ultrarational, eventempered character of their roles underlines the cruelty and irrationality of the young couple's fate. The play's last words, which they deliver, confirm as much:

MAN: In the past eight months the population of Ballymore has risen from
         13,527 to 13,569.

WOMAN: Life there goes on as usual.

MAN: As if nothing had ever happened. (88)

Yet while the Commentators' presence universalizes Joe and Mag's experience, places the moment of their innocent joy in the context of eternity, and
provides a judicious distance between emotional vitality and cold fact, there
is something not altogether satisfactory about them on an intellectual level.
Their relation to the theme is too static, too predetermined, too cerebral. The
interrelationship proposed between the play's two couples has the effect of reducing Joe and Mag's intimate history to a moral platitude along the lines of
"they're happy now but it won't last; they'll never get away with it." As Cass
McGuire exemplifies, the challenge is to live. The irony that declares Joe and
Mag winners grates in its shrillness. The view that "Joe and Mag are winners
because death forestalls the corruption of love"[18] seems cold comfort indeed.

As already noted, *Losers* is a reworking of the short story, "The Highwayman and the Saint." The saint in question is Saint Philomena, to whom
Hanna Wilson's bedridden, pious mother has a particular devotion. The
highwayman in the story is the eponymous figure in a frequently antholo-
gized period piece by the English poet Alfred Noyes (1880–1958). The
poem was recited by Andy Tracey, Hanna's boyfriend, during their close encounters on the Wilson couch. The sound of voices was necessary to reassure
Mrs. Wilson upstairs that all was decorously in order between the lovers. In
Losers the poem has been changed to Thomas Gray's "Elegy Written in a
Country Church-yard," but the short story's plot survives intact.

Care for her mother has prevented Hanna from marrying Andy and moving into his house. But circumstances at Andy's workplace force the issue.
The wedding takes place, but Andy moves in with the Wilsons, rather than
freeing Hanna from the emotionally paralyzing influence of her mother.
Andy, inspired by an Orangeman at work who reports from his newspaper
that Saint Philomena has been retired from the Church's roster of the elect,
summons up sufficient Dutch courage at the pub to break the news at home
and thereby break Mrs. Wilson's grip. Instead, he finds himself denounced
not only by his mother-in-law and her able acolyte from next door, Cissy
Cassidy, but also by his own wife. His bid for liberty makes his imprisonment
all the more secure.

The difference between the story and the play resides almost entirely in
differences in presentation. The story proceeds without quite such an empha-

sis on retrospection as the play. When the play opens, the story is already over, in effect: we find Andy replicating a habit of the deceased Mr. Wilson—looking at a brick wall with binoculars in the hope of seeing a bird. What follows is not only the unfolding of the narrative, but an interplay between the past of that narrative and the present denoted by the opening view of Andy. The present is contained in Andy's periodic commentaries on the past, and in order to maintain a fluid interrelationship between past and present in the audience's mind, the author's notes for the set request that there be "no attempt at a realistic division of the stage area, no dividing walls, no detailed furnishings: frames will indicate doors, etc., etc." (92).

Andy past and Andy present share the one chronology. Andy present, however, is now conscious in ways that Andy past repressed in the name of his emotional attachment to Hanna. "Well, I mean to say, anything for a quiet life" (141), he concludes, but this is with the knowledge of what happened the night he came home drunk, singing "God save Ireland" and gunning for St. Philomena. He now knowingly lends himself to Mrs. Wilson's unctious, self-serving prayer rituals, without Hanna's warmth to compensate him. His life as a man is at an end: Gray's "Elegy Written in a Country Church-yard" seems prophetic in retrospect.

Through his commentaries, Andy expresses an objective view of his situation and a fine grasp of the tissue of circumstances that enmeshed him. His experience obviates the necessity for impersonal commentators: unlike Joe and Mag, he is undeceived, and by his own efforts too. If "it is wrong to apply too far-reaching considerations"[19] to *Losers,* this emphasizes the completeness of Andy's isolated individualism, whose enemies are the play's three institutions: Church, family, and marriage. In order to survive, he has to learn to pretend to be duped into acceptance of and identification with all three. Clearly Andy's condition gestures mutely to that of Joe and Mag, and taken together *Winners* and *Losers* amount to more than the sum of their parts. But if the handling of the material is too inert in *Winners,* the material itself is too thin in *Losers.* And while the latter's title suggests that the play contains more than one loser, it does not adequately articulate what that means. In general, an audience will readily see the point of *Lovers,* but will be hard put to it to experience that frisson of recognition and insight that results from the persuasive embodiment of a dramatic idea.

Crystal and Fox

The sense of creative release and restless experimentation inaugurated by *Philadelphia, Here I Come!* finds its most enigmatic expression in *Crystal and*

Fox. This play, first produced at the Gaiety Theatre, Dublin, on 12 November 1968, has been thought a new departure for Friel. In terms of setting and personnel, it certainly seems novel. At the same time, it is connected to its predecessors by strong thematic and intellectual links.

Like most of Friel's protagonists, the central figures of *Crystal and Fox* are socially marginal. Fox Melarkey and his wife, Crystal, are the proprietors and professional mainstays of a travelling theater company—a "gaff" or fit-up show, once common in provincial Ireland. They have no permanent home; they spend most of their public lives pretending to be what they are not; they do the best business at the sites of public catastrophes. It is clear that they are firmly placed at the critical intersection of illusion and reality. And it is equally clear that Fox is determined to shear away illusion in an attempt to inhabit reality.

His means of doing so are destructive. The play opens with two theatrical deceptions. One is the close of their dramatic offering *The Doctor's Story,* a melodrama whose bathos and banality are reinforced rather than redeemed by its happy ending. The other is the fraudulent raffle, or lottery, in which the winning ticket is held by Papa, Crystal's father. Fox despises both performances, and no sooner have they concluded than he arbitrarily fires two of the company's leading players, El Cid and Tanya. This is the latest in a long line of firings, but it gives the departing Cid an opportunity to characterize Fox and to predict the likely course of events: "I know him—watched him since I joined this lousy fit-up—twisted, that's what he is—twisted as a bloody corkscrew! . . . And I'll tell you something more about him: he's not going to stop until he's ratted on everybody!"[20]

Fox has been in this destructive frame of mind, Crystal says, since their son, Gabriel, "went away" (35)—according to Gabriel himself, however, "he threw me out" (61). Yet Gabriel's return from England seems to dispel temporarily some of Fox's misanthropy: "Jaysus, but it's good to see you, son. After you went away, somehow we . . . we . . . But now you're back to us and suddenly life's . . ." (62). However, Gabriel turns out to be even more of a marginal than his parents and in his role of outsider has the unwitting effect of providing Fox with the opportunity for his ultimate act of destruction.

Gabriel has come home because he has committed robbery with violence on a defenseless old shopkeeper and is on the run from the law. Fox wishes to protect Crystal from this unsavory reality, but Gabriel gives her an incomplete version of it, with the result that Crystal offers him the shelter of "the show" (95) as a means of evading the law. But Gabriel does not manage to evade the law for long; the reality of its strong arm invades the players' encampment in the form of two brutal detectives. The reason that Gabriel has been found is revealing. Shortly after his arrival, Papa is taken to hospital. In order to protect himself, Gabriel will not go to visit him. Papa—lonely, worried, and vulnerable—keeps wondering aloud about Gabriel's absence, and word of this wondering eventually reaches the police. Gabriel's lack of emotional commitment, it seems, makes things worse for himself, not deliberately but—more mysteriously—by accident. The element of emotional cruelty here in Gabriel's behavior is reinforced by being made to coincide with Fox's deliberate strangulation of Gringo, the performing dog who is the sole source of creature comfort to its owner, Pedro.

Not surprisingly, Pedro leaves, reducing the company to the Melarkey family. And the company is soon reduced to Crystal and Fox, since it is after the Pedro incident that Gabriel is arrested. Fox now decides that the best thing to do is sell the company to raise money for Gabriel's defense. Once the sale has taken place, he and Crystal will be back where they started, as innocent, playful, and in love and Joe and Mag in *Winners*—as Fox says, "heaven's just round the corner" (123). But even this is not enough to satisfy him. Dawdling by the roadside pretending to hitchhike to Dublin so as to get to Manchester for Gabriel's trial, Fox perpetrates his final destructive act. He tells Crystal that it was he who betrayed Gabriel to the police to get the reward money. Crystal leaves him, and though Fox calls after her, truthfully, that he has lied, it is too late. He has finally succeeded in his desire to shatter all illusions. Having done so, he finds that he has nothing left.

It will be seen that *Crystal and Fox* is very elaborately plotted for a Friel play. It is also the playwright's most intellectually integrated and cerebral work to date, bringing together in one conclusive statement much of his earlier thinking about public and private lives, about the emotional minefield of family and interpersonal relations, about illusion and reality and the theatre as a metaphor that makes those two terms interchangeable and interdependent. Finally, this play faces with an uncharacteristic austerity and economy questions of chance, fate, and control. It is possible to consider *Crystal and Fox* a culmination of sorts in Friel's career, since it is the last play of his to be carried by a single character. From now on, his plays will consider groups in such a way as to emphasize ensemble playing.

Part of the meaning of *Crystal and Fox* is that it belies its title in interesting ways. Fox is by far the play's most significant character. But in order to attain a sense of his significance he feels obliged to write off what Crystal is in his life. Friel, through his title, insists on the combination of Crystal and Fox, on the combination of offsetting elements that the names connote—Crystal suggesting transparency and purity, Fox suggesting cunning and something untamed. At war with his context throughout the play—when Gabriel, on his return, asks how his father is, Crystal says, "The same Fox. Fighting the world" (60)—he finally abandons context, leaving him with his own revealed nature, the nature that constitutes his own singular reality, the nature which has deprived itself of "my Crystal . . . the only good part of me" (104).

The question of motivation, which has exercised some critics with regard to the play, therefore seems irrelevant. Robert Hogan on the whole considers the play "almost masterly" in its "absorbing portrait of a man who bit by bit dismantles his company and his life." But "nowhere in the play does Friel answer with sufficient theatrical clarity the central question posed by the action—why does Fox so inexorably, masochistically do this?"[21] According to Ulf Dantanus, "the problem is that Friel turns Fox into a character who threatens to step out of the realistic convention in an otherwise realistic play."[22] It may be argued, of course, that the play is not particularly realistic—for example, how the police happen onto Gabriel does not seem particularly plausible. In addition, since Fox has already reassured Gabriel, "I'm not much, sonny, but I'm no informer," (87) is it likely that Crystal, who presumably knows him better, will believe that he is?

Such questions, and problems with Fox's motivation, may be resolved by drawing attention to the parable-like character of the play. *Crystal and Fox* does not address the circumstantial travail of Mr. Fox Melarkey, private citizen, in the manner of such plays as *To This Hard House* or even *Losers*. Instead, it portrays a character in pursuit of an absolute definition of himself. If he has a motive for doing so, it is not one that he can articulate very well. His behavior comes not from a set of individualized feelings, therefore, but from a set of compulsions that, though vividly embodied by Fox, are not peculiar to him. From various remarks that he makes, however, and from one of the text's most prominent motifs, it is clear that if Fox is, as Crystal says, "fighting the world," he has pitted himself against two of its more immutable and problematic attributes, time and chance.

For Fox Melarkey, individual, spouse, father, and showman, the struggle is with time, as various remarks about change (whereby the passage of time is registered in personal terms) indicate. He tells Gabriel, "Things have changed all right; audiences, artists. Strange. You'd be surprised. The years do strange things to a man. But I have my Crystal" (64). He confesses to being "more perverse, more restless and more . . ." (64); more prone to change, that is, because "a man with a restlessness is a savage bugger" (68). Change seems to be not only desirable but necessary when one is, as Fox declares, "weary of all this . . . this making do, of conning people that know they're being conned. Sick of it all. Not sick so much as desperate; desperate for something that . . . that has nothing to do with all this" (68). "Once, maybe twice in your life, the fog lifts, and you get a glimpse, an intuition; and suddenly you know that this can't be all there is to it—there has to be something better than this" (102): these lines sum up Fox's awareness of his own inner turmoil.

Yet he has a vague idea of what might give him peace, what that "something better" might be: "What do I want? I want . . . I want a dream I think I've had to come true. I want to live like a child. I want to die and wake up in heaven with Crystal. What do I want? Jaysus, man, if I knew the answer to that, I might be content with what I have" (69). As this speech's pattern of tentativeness and questioning suggests, Fox is somewhat in a fog. Yet the dream he mentions comes within reach. If he does not quite end up in heaven, he reaches a state where "heaven's round the corner," a state which is a return to when "there'll just be you and me and the old accordion and the old rickety wheel—all we had thirty years ago, remember? You and me. And we'll laugh again at silly things and I'll plait seaweed into your hair again. And we'll go only to the fairs we want to go to, and stop only at the towns we want to stop at, and eat when we want to eat, and lie down when we feel like it. And everywhere we go, we'll know people and they'll know us—'Crystal and Fox!'" (123).

Crystal is central to the dream. She is the objective correlative by means of which Fox can fantasize about the reversal (and hence defeat) of time. Crystal sustains that role not only by her presence but because her presence lends itself to evaluation along the following lines:

> FOX: . . . How d'you think she's looking?
>
> GABRIEL: No change.
>
> FOX: No change at all. She is my constant enchantment.

And for all his destructiveness throughout the play, Fox maintains a line of amorous patter with Crystal, speaking what D. E. S. Maxwell has called "the actor's patois,"[23] to which Crystal responds in like manner. But the ostensibly spurious character of their exchanges does not mean their love has been illusory. In her absence, Fox tries to explain his final rejection of her by claiming "love alone isn't enough" (145). This may be the ultimate in destructive thinking; it may be the outcome of his trying "to stop myself but I couldn't" (145) from lying about his betrayal of Gabriel. All we know at the end of the play, is that without love there is only "the old rickety wheel" that Fox clutches during his closing lines.

Without love, it seems, there is only blind chance—the unplanned event that brings Gabriel back, the lottery that the suckers in the audience of *The Doctor's Story* fall for, the accidental words that lead to Gabriel's arrest. Clearly, in their blindness, in their befogged, inscrutable nature, such events are the enemies of dreams and freedom. Not surprisingly, Fox believes "the whole thing's fixed" (146). Yet, perhaps because of the pain of this perception, Fox concludes in a more understanding, gentler vein than he has hitherto been able to command: "But who am I to cloud your bright eyes or kill your belief that love is all. A penny a time and you think you'll be happy for life" (146).

Because of its intermingling of personal experience and generalized conditions, the play can be considered a parable of the human condition, a meditation on time, fate, illusion, imperfection. Yet it is also a dynamic piece of theater, containing some wonderful examples of timing and, by virtue of its uncharacteristically spare language, allowing its meaning to emerge as best it can from the introverted nature of the action, asking of its audience the stoical patience that it demands of its characters, and which Crystal almost embodies.

The Mundy Scheme

The Mundy Scheme is a direct contrast to *Crystal and Fox*. It was first produced at the Olympia Theatre, Dublin, on 10 June 1969, having been originally offered to the Abbey Theatre, which turned it down, considering it too controversial. This decision places the Abbey in the unflattering light of appearing to be a bastion of political and cultural sobriety and defensiveness.

It is not difficult to see why the play was thought controversial—one need look no further than its subtitle, *May We Write Your Epitaph Now, Mr. Emmet?* The reference is to a celebrated speech from the dock given on the eve of his execution in 1803 by Robert Emmet, leader of an abortive rebellion against English rule in Ireland in the same year. Emmet concludes his speech as follows: "Let no man write my epitaph: for, as no man who knows my motives dares now vindicate them, let not prejudice or ignorance asperse them. Let them and me repose in obscurity and peace, and my tomb remain uninscribed until other times and other men can do justice to my character; when my country takes her place among the nations of the earth, then, and not until then, let my epitaph be written."[24] As *The Mundy Scheme* reveals, the subtitle's question is ironic. Rather than become a nation, the country is in the process of being turned into a graveyard.

The play opens with a prelude in which an unseen voice focuses the subject at hand. The voice begins with serious-sounding questions—"What happens to an emerging country [Ireland] after it has emerged?"[25]—and proceeds by a series of mocking half-truths to the suggestion that what follows represents efforts made "to create the nation that the idealists of 1916 would have been proud of" (158).[26] What the play reveals is a farcical state of national affairs.

The play opens briskly with Roger Nash, the *taoiseach's* private secretary (the nearest English equivalent of *taoiseach* is *prime minister*), expertly disposing of his boss's correspondence by mimicking his platitudinous responses in a variety of tones. The quick-fire verbal and theatrical style of the play has been set. The reason Nash deals with the correspondence is that the taoiseach himself, F. X. Ryan, is indisposed with "a recurrence of his old trouble, labyrinthitis . . . sudden bouts of dizziness and nausea" (160). He soon puts in an appearance, however, to begin to make last-ditch efforts to save his government's and his party's faces—not to mention his forlorn hope of doing something to improve the country's social and economic conditions.

There is little to be done. Boyle, the minister of finance, has received the cold shoulder yet again from the financial wizards of Zurich. The only possibility of economic redemption is to accept an offer from the United States government to create nuclear submarine bases in West of Ireland ports. But this offer has already been rejected as a matter of principle, as Ryan explains: "Whatever small strength we have is in our absolute neutrality" (176)—though he does go on to remark that the ports in question are too small (which makes it easy to have principles). And as if things are not bad enough, the minister of foreign affairs is missing. The interview with Boyle culminates in an attack, relief from which is provided by Ryan's mother (with whom he lives)—the play is set in the taoiseach's residence.

Eventually the minister of foreign affairs, Michael Maloney, materializes, bringing with him the nation's salvation, the Mundy Scheme. The proposal, brainchild of Texan Irish-American Homer Mundy, is to turn the barren and depopulated wastes of the West of Ireland into an international burial ground. Given the price of real estate in the world's capital cities, and the amount of work it would give in Ireland, the scheme seems irresistible. It does meet with token resistance, however, since what is being contemplated is a totally opportunistic subletting of that part of the country enshrined in Ireland's modern cultural mythology as the homeland of the native. Once it is appreciated that benefits to personal bank balances will accrue to those in favor of the scheme, scruples evaporate.

The last two of the play's three acts present the scheme's implementation, replete with public apologetics on the one hand, and an epidemic of behind-the-scenes backstabbing, self-interest, and blackmail on the other. The play ends rather weakly with Ryan, assured of political survival, watching the inauguration of the burial grounds on television in the company of his cronies. Friel has seldom been more blatant in his dramatic exploitation of public and private lives. Indeed, his caustic satire of Irish public life, dedicated as it is here to the unprincipled politics of the highest bid, makes his recent elevation to the Irish Senate ironic. Hardly an aspect of political culture in the modern Republic of Ireland is allowed to pass unscathed, from the Irish version of Momism (Ryan living with his mother) to the eager sale of birthright when the price is right. Cultural shibboleths, such as the Irish equivalent of *patria o muerte* (fatherland or death), nativism, an unhealthy or at least dependent reliance on American get-rich-quick schemes, a facile replacement of public trust at the hint of private gain—all come in the way of a verbal demolition job.

The Mundy Scheme is among Friel's most verbally exuberant works, taking particular relish in exposing the typically duplicitous quality of politicians' speech. Here is the end of Maloney's sales pitch to the Cabinet, and the opening of Ryan's response:

MALONEY: Gentlemen, our country is in agony. And it seems to me we have two alternatives. We can say: we abdicate, we resign, we have run out of ideas and dedication, we have nothing more to give. Or, gentlemen, we can say: Ireland, I stand by you, I will see you through your labor, I will nurse you back to health and vigor and glory. The choice is ours, gentlemen. If our economy were buoyant, the Mundy Scheme would still be welcome. As it is, I think it is nothing short of miraculous. Thank you.

RYAN: Thank *you*, Mick. A very calm and very informative exposition. (225–226)

Despite its seemingly festive pugnacity, the play expresses a good deal of unease about the quality of public life in the Republic. The fact that it does little more than express it is part of the play's problem. There is too little differentiation between the characters, and in a sense the play depoliticizes itself by being too consistent. Indeed, Friel himself has said, "I submitted the play [to the Abbey] with the gravest misgivings and little enthusiasm."[27] Most critics tend to agree with D. E. S. Maxwell's appraisal: "Perhaps the immediate vehicle of the satire is too absurd."[28] It is probably true to say that *The Mundy Scheme* is more a symptom of its own political era than a candidate for permanent inclusion in the repertory of late-twentieth-century Irish drama. At the same time, though, it is an early rehearsal of Friel's eventual address to public themes, as well as being noteworthy for being conceived more for an ensemble than for a single protagonist and attendants.

The Gentle Island

Friel's next play, first produced at the Olympia Theatre, Dublin, on 30 November 1971, is so obviously a contrast to *The Mundy Scheme* as to suggest that the playwright deliberately meant it that way. *The Gentle Island* is set as far away from the farcical behavior of politicians as possible. It contains nothing of cultural commentary. Its central figure is a woman. And it has a remote, rural setting—the island in question is Inishkeen, off the coast of Donegal.

The play opens with an unusual sequence, a self-consciously deliberate ending to human community on Inishkeen. On the basis of a vote, the islanders have decided to abandon their home for the economic opportunities of the British mainland. The exceptions are the Sweeney family, consisting of patriarchal, one-armed Manus; his son Philly and Philly's wife Sarah; and a younger son, Joe. Philly is an inexpressive, hard-working fisherman, whom Sarah, in the course of the play, indicates has been sexually crippled by the presence of his powerful father. Joe, the play's one minor character, is volatile and uncertain as to whether his best interests lie in joining his girlfriend in London or in remaining with the family in the hope that the island will somehow return to its former life.

For the time being, however, the Sweeneys are lords of all they survey. Joe calls his father "King of Inishkeen," adding, "King of nothing."[29] Yet conditions are such as to raise inevitable questions of leadership, self-sufficiency, cooperation, and independence. This family is literally out on its own, to work out its destiny with only the promptings of its own dynamics to live by. Not only have the Sweeneys been desocialized, but Manus and Philly, the family's two most powerful members, seem critical of or at best indifferent to the social opportunities now available to those who voted for exodus. Philly's long-term plan for escape, stated in response to his wife's "I don't want to stay here" (16) seems to have rather less conviction than Manus's boast, "We're a self-contained community here" (24).

These words are addressed to the other two characters in the play, Shane and Peter. Their presence, obviously, disproves Manus's claim. Moreover, they represent a blatant antithesis to rural remoteness and family unity. Shane and Peter are Dubliners, homosexual lovers, and tourists, and ultimately they embody one of the clearest examples in Friel's plays of the unmasking effects of which outsiders are capable. Under a cloudless sky the relationship between the two parties proceeds ineluctably, though imperceptibly, to a shattering climax.

The focus of the plot's development is Sarah, who finds Shane's vitality, quirkiness, and capacity for zany behavior most attractive. To say that she is hurt by his rejection of her is a sizeable understatement. The rejection is the most obvious motive for her telling Manus that Shane and Philly are having sex, and "if you're the great king of Inishkeen, you'll kill them both" (62). And in the event, it is Sarah who fires the gun and leaves Shane a cripple. The physical emphases of the plot, not to mention the irruption of gunfire, is clearly a departure for Friel. It is important, however, not to be misled by the somewhat melodramatic plot into thinking that it carries the play's burden of thought. *The Gentle Island* may also be analyzed in terms proposed by D. E. S. Maxwell's view that "it is a parable of human groping after communion and permanence, and the elisions of contact that frustrate it."[30] Moreover, the play's end comes not with the shot that disables Shane, but with a conspiracy of silence concerning it (a conspiracy to which Philly is not a party), underlining its subsidiary, yet perhaps more telling, considerations of revelation, secrecy, truth-telling, masking, and ultimately of language.

Manus prepares Shane to be confronted with Sarah's allegations by telling him what Shane calls "an obscene story" (68) about the wanton torture of a previous visitor, a packman (similar no doubt to the one in the short story "Mr. Sing My Heart's Delight") who had been accused of robbing his island host. The story performs a number of functions in the context. Not for the first time in the play, attention is drawn to the exemplary power of narrative. Secondly, it is a reminder of the islanders' violent heritage. In addition, the story reveals once again the irrational and destructive manner in which outraged feeling may express itself.

When Manus then makes a tentative, menacing connection between the packman's alleged thievery and Sarah's allegations (or story) about Shane and Philly, one of Shane's responses is to break into a soft-shoe shuffle and stage-negro patter. This response may be Shane's means of not taking the confrontation seriously, or it may be because he doesn't know how seriously to take it. Shortly thereafter, now realizing that he must seriously defend himself, there is the following exchange:

SHANE: She's hysterical.

SARAH: I seen you! I seen you!

SHANE: (To MANUS.) For God's sake you don't heed her, do you?

SARAH: Ask him is it true? Ask him! Ask him!

SHANE: *She* wanted to sleep with me.

SARAH: With that thing, Manus! Is it the truth or is it a lie? (69)

Events earlier in the play confirm that Shane is telling the truth about Sarah's desire for him. Earlier events, when Sarah tells the true story of how Manus lost his arm, identify her as somebody who does not take readily to romantic stories that disguise the truth. Shane's "nigger minstrel" routine is a reprise of a much more elaborate performance in the same idiom earlier, a performance which also comes to an end in violence; a performance that is simply one of a series in the course of the play—Sarah tells him, "You're like the one on the radio, half the time I don't know what you be talking about" (30). Shane is also the one who flippantly tells Peter, "I hate choices" (20), and in an equally flippant manner: "If one admits that there is no absolute truth . . ." (32). The latter statement is echoed in Manus's statement following Sarah's unmasking of how he was mutilated: "There's ways and ways of telling every story. Every story has seven faces" (56).[31]

Undoubtedly this is so. But Manus's story occurs in the context of the others' stories. It is at least arguable that one of its faces will gaze on its reflection in the story of another. Thus it may be seen that when the story of Manus's arm turns out to be concerned with emotional deprivation rather than, as he would have it, mining in Montana, the truth of the former version is reflected in Sarah's unreciprocated sexuality. As Manus was maimed in the name of neglecting his wife, so too does Philly's neglect disable him. And while it remains difficult to authenticate "absolute truth," there is, in the meantime, the truth of need, which Sarah experiences, a truth so fundamental that to deny it and the love that is its spokesman is to deny life itself.

The primitive character of Sarah's inner reality makes her of her native island and at the same time helplessly and unwittingly in opposition to it. As the play's opening makes clear, life in the productive, familial, communal sense of the term is no more on Inishkeen. This state of affairs leaves the Sweeneys to face their lives together deprived of a bonding ethos. The opposite of such an ethos is violence—not simply in the argument of the play, but even more simply in considering what primitive part of the human makeup connotes the violence, destruction, and sundering that are love's antitheses. And violence ensures that Manus, Sarah, and Philly are tied together more indissolubly than ever by the end of the play. The only change that has occurred is an intensification of the status quo. The intervention of the two artistically inclined outsiders—Peter, the sentimental seeker of emotional permanence, is a musician; Shane's thespian proclivities bring energy and

color to an otherwise lifeless environment—has unforgettably clarified life
for the Sweeneys by defining its terminal, sterile character. They remain as
embedded in their reality as the Three Monks, the rocks in the island harbor
that, legend has it, represent what became of two young monks attempting
to escape their island habitat in the company of a beautiful young woman
(26–27).

As in *Crystal and Fox,* Friel is arguing in *The Gentle Island* that the world of
circumstances exists as the basis and pretext for the uncovering of the self's
fundamental character. Merely to make such a statement about two late
1960s Friel plays suggests how much his work developed in the dozen years
since he took to playwrighting. The development can be seen in his more
elaborate conceptions of theme and narrative structure. And although *The
Gentle Island* lacks the dramaturgical novelty of some of its immediate forerunners it lacks nothing of their technical competence. In addition, and perhaps most noticeably, Friel's language as a playwright has become a supple,
vital element in his work—not merely in his willingness to indulge language's histrionic and pyrotechnical capacities (which are typically indulged
in order to reveal their essentially illusionistic nature) but in terms of spare-
ness, directness, understatement, and rhythmic patterning. Had Friel abandoned the theater at this point in his career, he would already have earned his
place in the annals of mid-twentieth-century Irish theater, thanks largely to
Philadelphia, Here I Come!, The Loves of Cass McGuire, and *Crystal and Fox.*
It could be argued that by this point in his career Friel was such an accomplished dramaturge that his material was in danger of becoming cerebral and
recondite. In the plays of the next decade, Friel found a focus for the more existential and intellectual concerns that are never far below the surface of the
works discussed in this chapter. Far from abandoning the theater, Friel was
yet to produce his best work.

Chapter Four
All the World's a Stage

The production of *The Gentle Island* brought to an end the first phase of Friel's career as a playwright of note, both internationally and, more particularly, in Ireland. It is somewhat artificial, however, to speak of phases of Friel's career, since his output is at least as significant for its continuities as it is for its diversity (to use terminology that describes each individual Friel play). Thus, the plays of the 1970s remain faithful to, and articulate to an increasingly fine-tuned pitch, the playwright's original concerns. The divisions and commitments already analyzed are more intensely present in the plays about to be discussed. Friel's dramaturgical restlessness and interest in stage experimentation are as much to the fore as ever, and are arguably a more urgent presence than previously. Thematically, Friel continues in the 1970s to write about the family, about love, about illusion, about language, and perhaps above all about situations in flux, endings, beginnings, disorientations, and the turning of tides in the affairs of all too mortal men.

The later plays depart from the earlier plays in their settings and the meaning ascribed to, or implied by, these settings. As has been noted in connection with *Crystal and Fox* and *The Gentle Island,* social considerations enter the dramatic matrix only to the extent that they impinge on the more crucially existential concerns of those works. A similar case could be made for *Philadelphia, Here I Come!* and the other plays already discussed. It is as though, having tried unsuccessfully to provide something like sociological verisimilitude in the unpublished plays, Friel steered clear of such preoccupations, dealing instead with the inner man, the creature of conscience, spirit, and emotional need. This character's prototype is Columba in *The Enemy Within,* Friel's first successful play. Friel is not insensitive to social issues in his 1960s plays; still, the worlds of such protagonists as Fox Melarkey and Cass McGuire attempt to resist the powerful influence of social factors on the formation of their consciousnesses. Cass and Fox bear out Friel's early view of the role of playwrights: "They have this function: they are vitally, persistently, and determinedly concerned with one man's insignificant place in the here-and-now world. They have the function to portray that one man's frustrations and hopes and anguish and joys and miseries and pleasures with all the

75

precision and accuracy and truth that they know; and by doing so help to make a community of individuals."[1]

The challenge for Friel, therefore, if his work was to grow in scope and range, consisted in turning his thoughts away from enclaves as ostensibly self-contained as Iona, Ballybeg, Eden House, Inishkeen, and Fox's traveling show. As noted in chapter 3, *The Mundy Scheme* conceivably signals the beginning of such a development, since it can be seen as a critique of the self-sufficing, self-serving enclave of F. X. Ryan's home: to have the play's issues kept all in the family, as they seem to be, is one of the most obvious examples of how the public interest is being repressed. But *The Mundy Scheme* does not seem quite to realize all of its own potential.

On the other hand, critics have found that *The Gentle Island* "marks a new direction for Friel,"[2] as well as representing "the first suggestions of an attempt by Friel to dig deeper into the Irish psyche."[3] Its setting and its representation of the sexual component of interpersonal and family dynamics do extend Friel's range. The dramatic balance between the characters, however, along with Philly's anonymity, shows it to be a tentative development at best, particularly since its intellectual and emotional appeal has already been expressed with greater verve in *Philadelphia, Here I Come!* (in its treatment of the themes of isolation and emigration), *The Loves of Cass McGuire* (with its focus on the fate of women), and *Crystal and Fox* (which deals with emotional violence). In attempting to establish a pattern of development for Friel's career, therefore, it seems best to retain the argument that *The Mundy Scheme* and *The Gentle Island* are transitional pieces.

The transition is away from isolation toward the world. The world of the human is the world of society, the world of collective experience, the world of strangers. It impersonally registers itself through the names that denote collective experience and collective existence. Those names are history and culture. These, rather than the psyches of certain private individuals, now become the presences that demand unmasking. These areas now substantially comprise Friel's theater of interests; even the exceptions have an explicit historical and cultural dimension to them which influences their final outcome.

Such an enlargement of scope naturally has had its effect on the plays' structures. Much more so than previously, Friel is writing for an ensemble—as he begins to do in *The Mundy Scheme* and *The Gentle Island*—that functions as the inevitable technical outcome of the playwright's focus on collective experience. Friel has always implicitly understood and put into effect one of the hallmarks of "a Guthrie production," namely, "there were no 'extras,' no 'walk-ons,' they were all players, all essential to the play—no matter how small the part."[4] Now, however, he uses the ensemble to express his views on such terms in the lexicon of Irish politics and culture as *minority, power, language,* and *tradition.* Thus, his work in the 1970s shows Friel taking on the matter of Ireland, as many of his literary forebears have done. This commitment has also made his work richer, without compromising the values available to it from the earlier plays.

Friel's Theater of Fact

As a departure from his character-oriented origins in the theater, origins indebted to his formation as a story writer, Friel in his next phase as a dramatist deals with the world of facts. And in order to do so he evolves a mode of writing for ensembles, since facts are not the property of any one character but a convention whose reliability depends on there being more than one witness willing to testify to it.

The convention of facticity, therefore, has implicit associations of the collective and the social. To make the codes that govern the collective experience of Ballybeg, or any other culture, Friel has to turn the artistic tables on himself. In Friel's next two plays, *The Freedom of the City* and *Volunteers,* the characters, instead of being conceived from the inside (or placed in conditions where they must do so for themselves), are regarded externally. They attain significance not so much, or not primarily, in terms of resistance to those codes as by denoting how the codes have shaped them, and how little independence the codes permit. Corollaries of this development are Friel's increasing awareness of how limited current conceptions of individuality are, and his correspondingly increasing anger and bitterness at such limitation, particularly when responsibility for it can be laid at the door of some fact-dealing social institution.

An equally important development, based on this presentation of character, is the increased intellectual commitment of these plays. This development can be seen in a variety of ways. Indeed, one of the ways of thinking about Friel's work from *The Freedom of the City* onward is to study the influence of a new conceptual terminology on the older one retained from the earlier plays. In other words, while such abstractions as love, time, chance, and fate continue to hold their prominent positions in Friel's thinking, other concepts with a more obviously social application, such as justice, alienation, class, and the past, are also in evidence. (In the case of both sets of concepts, their presence is felt precisely because it is latent, tacit, offering forms of discourse not availed of by the characters but which might well be useful to an audience willing to participate in the collective experience of the play in terms it understands.) Coinciding with this development, but not deriving from it, is the serious critical attention Friel's plays from this juncture onwards begin to command.

Finally, and as a direct outcome of his larger, or perhaps more pragmatic, intellectual commitment, Friel subverts the theater of fact once he has established it. His doing so anticipates another shift of emphasis later on in his career, from theater of fact to a theater of language. In *The Freedom of the City* and *Volunteers* the significance of the subversion derives precisely from the fact that both plays have been inspired by contemporary historical events—events, that is, whose factual character there is no denying. Both plays show that what passes for fact is a social and cultural construct: it is the inscription of a code collectively assented to by various institutional interests. The power to make the claims of each particular code hold good and the destructive effect on those who have little or no institutional interests are the sources of conflict in *The Freedom of the City* and *Volunteers*, and offer the playwright a means of embodying the various agents that tarnish the human image and of upholding the dignity of that image.

The Freedom of the City

Nothing in Friel's output is a rehearsal for *The Freedom of the City,* first produced at the Abbey Theatre, Dublin, on 20 February 1973 and given a concurrent production at the Royal Court Theatre, London, where it opened on 27 February 1973 under the direction of the noted English actor Albert Finney.

The play's originality within the Friel canon is due to its urban setting, to its concern with social class, to its derivation from contemporary historical events in Derry, a human community whose modern character differs so profoundly from that which inspired the love of its patron saint, Columba. It may be argued that *"The Gentle Island* is not only about Inishkeen. Ireland has been historically, and is, a violent land."[5] Leaving aside the point that the relationship between history and violence is not peculiar to Ireland, the gunfire in *The Gentle Island* is merely a muffled aberration compared to that heard in *The Freedom of the City,* a freedom now articulated with the full force of the irony so crudely handled in *A Sort of Freedom.*

Part of the reason that nothing prepares the student of Friel for *The Freedom of the City* is that there was no possible means of anticipating the events upon which it draws.[6] On 30 January 1972, subsequently known as Bloody Sunday, thirteen members of a civil rights protest march in Derry were shot and killed by members of the British Army.[7] Though this was not the first violence inflicted on civil rights supporters in Northern Ireland, its scale shocked the country. The shock was not diminished when the findings of the official (British) tribunal exonerated the military.

Friel's play has a twofold approach. It presents a naturalistic portrait of the victims and of their various though related embodiments of what the term *civil rights* means. In addition, and inhibiting a clear view of that portrait, there is a schematized model of various reactions to the events—including a version of the tribunal hearings and of various unrelated attempts to provide a framework of understanding for the social trauma that has taken place. Besides the various officials and witnesses participating in the hearings, those offering a framework of understanding are an American sociologist, Dodds; a television commentator from the Irish Republic covering the victims' funeral, O'Kelly; an anonymous local priest; and an anonymous local balladeer and chorus. The three central characters, Lily, Michael, and Skinner, are flayed in the crosstalk of language from the various "framers" as surely as they are butchered by the soldiers' bullets.

The play opens with the worst already over: Lily, Michael, and Skinner have been killed. Without a word, the lighting then picks out "the JUDGE high up in the battlements," a complicated image relating both to the remoteness of the judge presiding over the tribunal hearings from the actual events and, more generally, to Derry's status as a walled city, a loyalist redoubt, synonymous in the language of Unionist mythology with intransigence. Thus the dramatic issue of the play is set and its complex conflicts adduced. These conflicts are between the mortal, earthbound victims and lofty, abstract justice, between violence and law, between ends and beginnings, between symbols and realities. From this stark intersection of contending images the play proceeds.

The events concerning the victims are as follows. Lily, Michael, and Skinner, participants in a demonstration for civil rights, find themselves disoriented and seeking shelter when the demonstration is broken up by troops using CS gas. The haven they secure with each other's help turns out to be no less than the lord mayor's parlor in Derry's Guildhall. Physical disorientation gives way to cultural unease as the nature of their whereabouts dawns on them. Yet they do not remain daunted. In fact, they have a field day, drinking the lord mayor's liquor, using his phone, smoking his cigars, wearing his official regalia and availing of his toilet facilities. Within this temporary and unlikely shelter they assume the freedom of the city. (The play's title is the name given to the bestowal of honorary citizenship on important guests, a ceremony dating from medieval times and still carried out in Europe. The play's action ironizes the sociocultural assumptions of such pomp and circumstance.) The trio's activities are a doomed, naive pantomime, which nevertheless contain at least as much human worth as the official mayoral ritual conferring the freedom of the city. It also puts into intimate, practical perspective the cry of the demonstration's keynote as the tanks bear down: "Stand your ground! . . . This is your city!"[8] The trio's fugitive freedom exists in the apparent no-man's-land between ritual and exhortation.

The freedom they assert is the freedom to constitute a miniature community, or family, the normative social keystone, with Lily taking the motherly role, a natural one, presumably, since she is the mother of eleven children. Michael and Skinner lend themselves to this enabling, humanizing fiction, as they do to others. In this respect, Michael seems the more obvious casualty of illusion. He retains a touching faith in social possibility; he is a slightly older version of Joe Brennan from *Winners*. Civil rights, for him, is a question of social mobility and stoicism: "As long as we don't allow ourselves to be provoked, ultimately we must win" (59). Reinforcing the bitter irony of such an attitude, Michael rehearses his companions for the aftermath of their escapade: "The thing to remember is that we took part in a peaceful demonstration. . . . Now, if they want to be officious, supposing they take our names and addresses, that's all they're entitled to ask for and that's all you're expected to give them" (81). Even in the moment of death (one of the play's most arresting strokes is to permit the three to articulate their own deaths), Michael's last words convey his faith in an ultimate rightness of things and how the bullets blast it: "My mouth kept trying to form the word mistake. . . . And that is how I died—in disbelief, in astonishment, in shock. It was a foolish way for a man to die" (71).

In contrast, Skinner, who throughout is antagonistic toward Michael and Michael's decent, petit-bourgeois, conformist aspirations, is the trio's voice of consciousness. Rootless, feckless, witty, potentially violent, he is at once most estranged from social advance and has the most provocative social perspective. He is the one who has no compunction in availing of the Guildhall's amenities; he is not averse to a bit of vandalism; Michael considers him the kind who will give the civil rights movement a bad name for rudeness and irresponsibility: "That Skinner's a trouble-maker. . . . I wouldn't be surprised if he was a revolutionary" (48). Skinner knows that he is not; his last words are, "I died, as I lived, in defensive flippancy" (72), acknowledging as his epitaph his lack of that "total dedication" possessed by the troops shooting him.

Michael lacks access to the social institutions that would ratify his good faith. Skinner denies himself the potentially freeing actions that might result from harnessing his insights to social objectives. He defines the civil rights movement for Lily: "It has nothing to do with doctors and accountants and teachers. . . . It's about us—the poor—the majority—stirring in our sleep" (77). It is left to Lily to occupy the middle ground, the unmediated human ground, untouched by but by no means ignorant of social climbing or alienation. Vaguely challenged by Skinner she admits that she marches for civil rights as a mark of respect and hope for her mongoloid son. Her perception of this reason for marching is that it is "stupid" (78), which Skinner denies.

Lily's story is the play's most obviously emotional expression of disenfranchisement. Thus it is also the play's most potent assertion of reinfranchisement, because it is its most unqualified statement of hope. Those whom society has evidently rejected and apparently feels it can dispose of with impunity occupy center stage in *The Freedom of the City*. Friel's gesture of rehabilitation, cultural solidarity, and optimism is as significant as any that Michael, Skinner, or Lily might make in the name of civil rights. Even if the freedom that, as Skinner tells Michael, they "presumed" (58) to confer on themselves is merely prelude to ultimate eclipse, an illusion of safety, it should not be devalued. Its value lies in its fragility, its presumptuousness, its spontaneity, and its playfulness.

Lily, Michael, and Skinner have been called "stock characters,"[9] but it is important to note that none of the juridical or cultural emporia represented in the play stock them. Neither the courts, the church, nationalist mythology, nor the mass media can find language that adequately recounts the trio's experience or its significance. Troops surround the Guildhall and order them out because they believe they number forty dangerous agitators—who else would be in an official building, whose reality consists of the symbolic freight it supports? Such a blatant distortion comes sufficiently late in the play for it to be part of the context of official, symbol-generating, distorting language. In this sense there seems little to choose between the language of the church, which places the trio among the meek who will inherit the earth; the language of nationalist mythology, which claims that they are martyrs; and the language of the courts, which identifies them as armed and dangerous, though this language has a particular social potency, since it has the institutional power to pass itself off as the language of fact and to make its verbiage synonymous with the language of truth.

All these idioms pay lip service to a network of generalized perceptions rather than testify to individuation and particularity. They also have the effect of distancing the trio's experience because they classify it. Yet, while the distancing is experienced, so too is the reciprocal effect of creating intimacy between the audience and the trio, since the audience cannot but perceive the transparent inadequacy of the various official languages.[10] The discrepancy is most provocatively and subtly embodied in the play's ostensibly most redundant character, Professor Dodds, the American sociologist.

Entering under his own recognizances, so to speak, and with no obvious ideological or institutional ax to grind, he seems superfluous to this already quite densely populated play. As in the case of Lily, who seems to be out of place but who represents the fundamental ground upon which all assumptions about society and community are built, Dodds comes the closest to establishing an objective understanding for the trio. At any rate there is a certain facile plausibility about formulations regarding "my field of study . . . inherited poverty or the culture of poverty or more accurately the subculture of poverty" (19). Yet the seductive fluidity of the professor's confident language does not disguise the generalizing and impersonalizing tendency in his approach. Ultimately his language is as suspect as the rest, since its objective is to assert a model for Lily, Skinner, and Michael to fit.

The alternative, of course, is to permit them the uncluttered freedom to evolve their own codes of denominating themselves and the world, a world they implicitly desire to speak to them in language they can understand. It never will, unless those willing to listen to such a language, Lily and Michael in particular, have some say in the pliability of its syntax.

While *The Freedom of the City* has its ostensible and immediate pretext, therefore, it exceeds the empirical limitations of its origins. Friel ensured that the play would be seen as a response to events, rather than a reproduction of those events, by introducing a distancing feature of his own: the play is set in 1970. Adapting such familiar components of his dramatic imagination as the relationship between public and private behavior, reality and illusion, hope and impoverishment, Friel has created for the stage a working model of a culture, represented by the trio, and a model of how a culture does not work, represented by the language of stereotype.

The play ends with a reading of the tribunal's findings. This is followed by a wordless interlude in which there is "a fifteen-second burst of automatic fire. . . . The three stand as before, staring out, their hands above their heads" (96). In this tableau, distance and closeness seem to act as one. Lily, Michael, and Skinner are arrested in the typical posture of the suspect. Yet they also seem to have withstood the force that would eliminate them. As suspects, they become distanced, alien, less than themselves. As survivors, they become moving, attractive, triumphant. The illusion of their survival is more humanizing than the reality of their execution. Friel's theater privileges the illusion in order that the humanizing option be kept alive.

Volunteers

With his next play, first produced at Abbey Theatre, Dublin, on 5 March 1975, Friel delves more deeply into the condition of modern Ireland by laying bare, as he did in *The Freedom of the City,* the connections and disconnections between violence, culture, and redemptive humanism.

Once again, contemporary events offered the playwright the basis for his anatomy of culture. In this case, Dublin is the setting, and the contemporary reference is to the Wood Quay affair, a controversy that arose when it was discovered that Dublin City Corporation intended to build an office block on the site of the original Viking settlement from which Dublin grew, one of the richest archaeological sites in Northern Europe.[11]

Friel once again enlarges his range in a number of noteworthy ways. Focusing on the past and present of the Irish capital enables him to underline the issues raised in the more localized *The Freedom of the City.* That play's use of the Guildhall as a temporarily credible but ultimately illusory image of safety and community is adapted in *Volunteers,* where the hole in which the work is carried out is partitioned from the ordinary citizenry and below the level of their daily activity, yet is all the more significant by being thus distanced. And, just as in *The Freedom of the City* Friel made his trio of social outsiders dramatic insiders (their fate being the core of the play), in *Volunteers* the play's issues are embedded in the behavior of a group of self-styled social rejects, whose collective title names the play. It may be that Friel's intention is to carry out "an excoriation of the Southern establishment;"[12] it also seems, however, that *Volunteers* sustains less narrow ambitions.

The second act of *The Freedom of the City* opens with the Balladeer, still drunk, intoning another mythologizing opus on behalf of "three Derry volunteers" (69)—Lily, Michael, and Skinner. The term *volunteer* has an illustrious place in the lexicon of Irish militaristic nationalism. It resonates with notions of sacrifice freely made and the values of disinterest, generosity, and independence of mind that are the antitheses of conscription's connotations. In the group of volunteers in the play, it is precisely such values that come under pressure.

The term gains additional resonance from the fact that these volunteers are in jail, "interned . . . because of attitudes that might be inimical to public security," as their spokesman, Keeney, says.[13] Presumably they voluntarily identified with such attitudes. They also volunteered for the dig, however, which has been in the nature of work release from prison, a gesture in the name of freedom that has made them marked men among their ideological comrades. The play's first act ends with Keeney informing his workmates that death awaits them in prison when the dig is completed. By this time they know that this is their last day on the job—the work is not finished, but construction of the hotel that is to be built on the site can wait no longer. It is out of the arbitrariness of such remorseless constraints that Friel fashions an image of human viability, an image that honors the values of voluntarism. Can something of value be saved from their enclosure in a workplace that "does look more like a bomb-crater—or maybe a huge womb—or . . . like a prison-yard with the high walls and the watch-tower up there and the naughty prisoners trying to tunnel their way out to freedom ha-ha-ha" (31)?

The speaker is Keeney, who single-handedly carries the play's momentum. His words mark the beginning of a brilliant, irreverent imitation of a school tour of the site, in which, as usual, his only slightly less witty partner, Pyne, participates. This two-man show is typical of the play. But it is important to notice the context in which it occurs. Keeney opens his tour as a specific distraction from two of his workmates, Knox and Butt, talking about the nocturnal screaming of the fifth member of the group, Smiler. The violent contrast between Keeney's act and Pyne's statement about Smiler—"It's almost every night now. Jesus, he must go through agonies" (31)—is typical of the play's shocking oscillations between moods and focal points. The erratic and unpredictable momentum thus engendered functions as an aggressively articulated tissue of freewheeling, improvisatory play notably at odds with the volunteers' doomed and captive circumstances.

Yet though the play's verbal pyrotechnics are among Friel's most spectacular, they do not override the play's seriousness. Smiler's story gets told. He is called Smiler because he wears a simpleton's grin and behaves like a simpleton. This behavior is the result of a beating he received leading a demonstration of striking workers. Smiler wears a mask of nonconsciousness because he has nothing to smile about. His is the pathos and the unmanned, degraded, unredemptive character of the victim. If Keeney talks back, acts out, indulges himself in the exuberance of his own verbosity, it is in order to express his difference from Smiler, to ensure that he remains aware and responsive and thus cannot lend himself to the emasculated status of victim. He is "quick-witted, quick-tongued, and never for a second unaware. Years of practice have made the public mask of the joker almost perfect" (18).

During the course of the play Smiler causes Keeney's mask to slip by disappearing from the worksite. This event brings about Keeney's revelation of their fate at the hands of their prison comrades. He has to reveal it in order to explain why he believes Smiler is better off at large. When Smiler returns, Keeney exclaims, "He's a stupid, pig-headed imbecile! . . . And that's why he came back here—because he's an imbecile like the rest of us!" (60). This expression of bitterness is a more aware expression of feeling than his comrades' more predictable and sentimental greetings, and is a more accurate reflection of the issues, to which once more it draws those comrades' less vigilant attention. The idiosyncracy of Keeney's responses authenticates his independence of mind, an embodiment of freedom that Keeney has not surrendered and that enables him to live in the present in a manner that does not devitalize or demoralize him.

Smiler is the onstage—therefore more definitive—embodiment of the values ascribable to Lily's Declan in *The Freedom of the City*. But he is not the play's only unlucky, uncomprehending victim. He represents in contemporary terms a condition that is age-old and that is defined by the presence in *Volunteers* of Leif, the Viking skeleton, whom Keeney and his men treat as an old friend. Who is Leif? Keeney rehearses some possible answers in the company of George, the site overseer, pointing to the remains' evidence of violence, still visible after perhaps a millennium: "What in the name of God happened to him? D'you think now he done it to himself? . . . Or maybe a case of unrequited love, George . . . ? Or maybe he had a bad day at the dogs? Or was the poor eejit just grabbed out of a crowd on a spring morning and a noose tightened round his neck so that obeisance would be made to some silly god. Or—and the alternative is even more fascinating, George—maybe the poor hoor considered it an honour to die—maybe he volunteered" (25–26).

Answers are perhaps less important than the attitude that keeps asking such questions, keeps trying to imagine (and by that means return to life, return to minds that are alive) Leif's fate. Later on, Pyne invents a history for Leif "out of the top of my head" (52), picturing him as a voyager to America who, inexplicably as far as Pyne is concerned, becomes homesick and returns home, to Dublin. Similarly, Smiler returned, for reasons he tries to explain and cannot.

Leif is also important because he inspires the one job that the volunteers are able to finish, his burial (Keeney's proposal, to which Smiler assents). If they do not pay their comrade-in-history this mark of respect, he will merely be the recipient of "hundreds and hundreds of tons of hard-core" (65). The burial is marked not by pomp and circumstance but by imitations of the kind of talk that attends such occasions, fond memories at first, followed by gossip and cutting down to size. Such common talk is more faithful to the place where Lief lies than more formal or ceremonial displays (such as the funeral in *The Freedom of the City*). Once again, as in everything in which Keeney takes a part, it is not a question of appropriateness, it is a question of attitude. In the case of Lief, it is instructive to compare the volunteers' attitude to the skeleton with that of some locals in a much more famous Irish play than *Volunteers,* J. M. Synge's *Playboy of the Western World,* where such remains are considered comically grotesque: "Did you never hear tell of the skulls they have in the city of Dublin, ranged out like blue jugs in a cabin of Connaught?"[14] Just as with Smiler, there is a great distance between the rest of the volunteers and Leif, and at the same time, there is no distance at all.

As Seamus Heaney has noted, Leif presents "a bony structure that can be fleshed with any number of possible meanings: a symbol, in fact, as is the thirteenth-century jug lovingly restored by the site foreman."[15] The foreman, George, thinks more of the jug than he does of Leif, or at least the cultural values the jug are conventionally thought to enshrine are, equally conventionally, considered to have little relation to Leif (a name chosen, presumably, because of its being an anagram for life). Such an attitude removes the jug from its habitat and context and confers on it the conclusive distance of a final resting place in a museum. George is even capable of overlooking the fact that were it not for the interest and enthusiasm of Butt there would be no jug. When George, however, as though in valediction, cautions Butt against Keeney, Butt drops the jug. This action, too, is inscrutable, deviant, totally unexpected—particularly since Butt has been the one volunteer apparently willing to play the establishment game in his eagerness to work and learn. When George, in what he presumably understands to be a gesture of good will, offers to become Butt's conscience, Butt reveals where he stands—with Keeney, with the kind of touch that Keeney represents, a touch that is creative rather than restorative: "anarchic" (47), as Keeney says, though he also perceives the inferiority of his own "paltry flirtations . . . fireworks that are sparked occasionally by an antic imagination" to Butt's "consistency" (57).

The echo of Hamlet's "antic disposition"[16] in Keeney's judgment of himself is not fortuitous. Hamlet, however, is not kept at a distance, another cultural trophy with Scandinavian associations. Rather, he is a figure who, like Leif, is more closely associated with the volunteers than with their custodians and enemies. Keeney makes this clear by repeating inexplicably, infuriatingly, and at most inopportune moments, the question, "Was Hamlet really mad?" In one sense, the question could not be more irrelevant or more remote from onstage concerns. As in other instances, however, remoteness disguises, or acts as a pretext for, intimacy; it is no more a definitive condition than anything else embodied by the volunteers (even Smiler acts unpredictably, by disappearing). Hamlet is available as a precedent, just as Lief is, a form requiring life and relevance to be conferred on him.

The truth of Hamlet is the truth of theater. Hamlet's assumption of various roles, his glib language, his feigning, and his courage (whereby his role is finally integrated) are all duly honored by the gamut of human behavior in *Volunteers*. As in *Hamlet*, betrayal and disloyalty are included in the gamut. Des, the volunteers' student supporter, cannot defend their need to complete the job to his superiors. He merely speaks the volunteers' language; he is unable to make influential the values upon which that language draws. Like Rosencrantz and Guildenstern, he is an unknowing dupe in a power struggle.

The question of Hamlet's madness is another of the play's inscrutable inquiries. Once again, the question is more important than the answer, since the question is, in effect, what is to be thought of the idea of Hamlet's madness? If, however, there is a point at which Hamlet seems not mad, it is in the gravediggers' scene: there his natural fellow feeling, prompted by memory and enhanced by love, proves sufficient. The reminders of mortality, his own and that of his fellow men, find Hamlet at his most engaging, at his most conversible.

In *Volunteers*, there is Keeney and the gravediggers. Keeney acts in open rebuke of a state in which there is something rotten (since it wants to speedily entomb its past): "He is a Hamlet who is gay, not with tragic Yeatsian joy but as a means of deploying and maintaining his anger."[17] But he is a Hamlet who must also care for his gravediggers, particularly since in this case a collective grave is being dug, in which will be buried anonymously the generosity, idealism, and quirkiness that animate these men and that sets them irrevocably apart from the prison that "Viking Ireland, like Denmark, is"[18]—and not only Viking Ireland, but also contemporary Ireland, as this "bitter . . . beautiful,"[19] and surprisingly neglected play asserts.

Return to Ballybeg

Friel's theater of fact could also be called his theater of criticism. Indeed, that label would be more accurate, in the sense that it would draw attention not simply to Friel's availing of contemporary events for dramatic purposes but to what validates his availing of them. His critique of standardized, conventionalized, institutionalized versions of truth is obviously much more significant, culturally and artistically speaking, than the fact of his having situated the critique in material of a strongly documentary character. The effect of this overtly critical disposition is developed in Friel's next two plays, *Living Quarters* and *Aristocrats*, where the documentary basis of the material is slight or nonexistent.

Having left Ballybeg for a wider stage (though that stage, in literal terms, is—for all its public scope—narrower, consisting of a room or a hole, and more seriously constraining), Friel returns to it for *Living Quarters* and *Aris-*

tocrats. His attitude to what Ballybeg connotes has now been modified by the plays written in the interval since *Crystal and Fox,* so that the effect of his return is that of demonstrating that Ballybeg is no longer tenable. (In two later plays, *Translations* and *The Communication Cord,* this conclusion is further demonstrated from a somewhat different standpoint than that of *Living Quarters* and *Aristocrats.*) In *Living Quarters,* those who cannot outgrow Ballybeg are fated to remain there. In *Aristocrats,* the final break is made— gently, perhaps sentimentally, but irrevocably. And as is revealed by these two plays taken together (it is interesting to note how Friel's plays seem to pair themselves off), the responsibility for implementing and learning from a critique of Ballybeg is the characters' own. This responsibility is not easily recognized, much less put into effect, and Friel is careful to imply in *Aristocrats* that it must not be forced, but must seem an inevitable outcome of time and circumstances. Nevertheless, the critical element in the play should not be considered incidental because it is not given a conspicuously revolutionary presence. On the contrary, its force is all the stronger for having apparently infused every aspect of the play's world.

One important effect of the joint embodiment of the theater of fact's critical spirit in *Living Quarters* and *Aristocrats* is to cause a reassessment of Friel's outsider figures. If the voice of a critique is to be heard in *The Freedom of the City* and *Volunteers,* it is in the characters of Skinner and Keeney. In *Living Quarters* and *Aristocrats,* the two outsider figures, Ben and Eamon, are much more emotionally involved with the action, and thus find it difficult to keep a judicious, critical distance from it. They are outsiders whose roles as such require the assistance of the rest of the characters, a subtle development by the author of this character type. Thus, in various ways, although *Living Quarters* and *Aristocrats* may seem a withdrawal on the part of the playwright from public themes, these plays have the effect of deepening and broadening what was valuable in his addressing those themes, the questioning spirit of the critique, the holding of a mirror up to potential rather than, as previously, up to nature.

Living Quarters

First produced at the Abbey Theatre, Dublin, on 24 March 1977, *Living Quarters* might seem a withdrawal to earlier Friel concerns, with its setting in Ballybeg, its concentration on home and family, and its questioning of the substance of love. Yet, as Seamus Deane has noted, it shares with its immediate contemporaries in the Friel canon "an interest in the disintegration of traditional authority and in the exposure of the violence upon which it has rested."[20]

Again, it is possible to assess this Friel play in terms of the relationships it establishes between public and private behavior. More particularly, *Living Quarters* emphasizes the clash between the predictability of professional duty and the complex, ungovernable, formless character of those areas that reside behind public roles. The play is careful not to place one of these areas above another. The heroism of Major Frank Butler, the central character, in rescuing his troops under fire is not belittled by the fact that he cannot exhibit the same kind of heroism under emotional fire at home, even though the failure destroys him. It is simply the case that there are different aspects of the human and no one individual can embody all of them with equal consistency. But what makes this case complex is that it takes an extraordinary shock to stimulate awareness of the limitations of one's own capacities. The stimulation of such an awareness is what leads to Frank's suicide in *Living Quarters;* and inasmuch as it does so, the play may be considered a critique of previous Friel embodiments of naturalness—all the more so since the critique emerges not so much from the course of a fateful evening's events as from the re-enactment of them in formal, conscious, artificial form from a script directed by the unreal but crucial Sir.

The play's plot centers around the reunion of the Butler family on the occasion of its head, Frank, being publicly congratulated and promoted for his gallant deeds in the Middle East (even here, Friel has availed of events in the news, namely the service of Irish troops during the mid-1970s in the United Nations Middle East peacekeeping force). Each of the family members seems defined by his or her emotional outlook: Helen lives unhappily in England; Miriam, in contrast, is a local wife and mother; Ben lives close by in an estranged state; and Tina, the youngest, still lives at home, emotionally innocent. They have not seen each other since their mother's funeral some time ago. In the meantime, life in the family home has changed: "middle-aged"[21] Frank has remarried. Anna, whom he idolizes, is in her "early twenties" (6). The revelation that, while Frank was on active duty, Ben and Anna had what she calls "our attempt at a love affair" (60) is the cause of the suicide.

The play addresses the question, What do such events mean? or, How is it possible to assign meaning to them? As his introductory remarks state, Sir and his ledger have been invented to arrive at understanding: "And in their imagination, out of some deep psychic necessity, they have conceived this *(ledger)*—a complete and detailed record of everything that was said and done that day, as if its very existence must afford them their justification, as if in some tiny, forgotten detail buried there—a smile, a hesitation, a tentative gesture—if only it could be found and recalled—in it must lie the key to an understanding of *all* that happened. And in their imagination, out of some deep psychic necessity, they have conceived me—the ultimate arbiter" (9–10). Sir, then, embodies a principle of coherence and integration, which is the opposite of the tendency toward dissolution and destruction in actual, so-called historical facts. The principle is real because of the need retrospectively felt for it by all concerned, a need created by the starkly inadequate compensations of memory.

Yet, with such a genesis, Sir is an inevitability, as his obdurate sticking to the ledger's script confirms. He is the recording angel who cannot alter the record, having no emotional investment in or subjective reading of its origins. But it is not merely in this sense that his presence is inevitable. It is because the Butler family is, in any case, even before the reunion's terrible climax, locked together in memory. All their talk together is of old times, childhood escapades, the pain of family conformity and the pain of breaking with it, and the inevitable emotional wounds that are endemic to the paradox of the familial—namely, families confer individuation by acts that are calculated. Hurt informs the story of Helen's failed marriage, a marriage destroyed by the tension of social class—her husband being Frank's batman (orderly), Gerry Kelly. Helen concludes her story: "I've lost him. She killed him. He's gone. Do I love Gerry Kelly still? I thought I'd squeezed every drop of him out of me. But now I know I haven't forgotten a second of him" (50).

The "she" incriminated in Helen's words is her mother, for years a cripple tended to by Frank. It is she who has cast a pall of emotional retribution on her children. Even Ben, "a mother's boy" (21) according to Miriam, confesses to Anna that immediately after her funeral, "suddenly I had to rush out of the room because I was afraid I'd burst out singing or cheer or leap into the air" (58–59), a feeling that is followed by being "guilty as hell . . . a guilty grief. All very strange" (59)—arguing for the perplexing strength of emotions released.

The play's most obvious example of such release and its confusion is, the abortive affair. But the most vocal tribute to release (and perhaps blindness to release's complexity) comes from Frank. As his name implies, he is a plain, blunt soldier, and after his first marriage cannot help but marvel at his good fortune with Anna, who is, as he tells Helen: "warm and open and refreshing. And so direct—so direct—so uncomplicated. Anything she thinks—whatever comes into her head—straight out—it must come straight out—just like that. So unlike us: measured, watching, circling one another, peeping out, shying back" (32–33). Yet Anna's real frankness and emotional generosity has dimensions to it that Frank cannot begin to suspect. One of Anna's effects on him is to reconsider the family's past: "Wondering have I carried over into this life the too rigid military discipline that—that the domestic life must have been bruised, damaged, by the stern attitudes that are necessary over—" (29).

As usual with Friel, syntax maketh man: the difficulty Frank has in communicating "what I was thinking" (29) suggests his unfamiliarity with this line of thought, the strangeness of this line of talk, and the fact that his mind and his language are not fully coordinated: he may mean well, but he is not in possession of the whole picture. But then, in the fractionalized world of *Living Quarters,* who is? Discounting Sir, who is the integer that the fractions potentially make up, the answer to this question is Anna. Not only is she different in ways Frank recognizes, she is different in ways of which he has never conceived, as, for instance, in the expression of her need of him during his official absence that precedes her confessing the affair: "And I tried to keep you, to maintain you in my mind—I tried, Frank, I tried . . . I searched Tina for you, and Miriam, but you weren't in them. And then I could remember nothing—only your uniform, the colour of your hair, your footstep in the hall . . . a handsome, courteous, considerate man . . . who wrote me all those simple, passionate letters—too simple, too passionate. And then Ben came. And I found you in him, Frank" (84).

The loneliness she speaks of, the consciousness of estranged love and her refusal to abide by its terms, are the all-too-human connection and disconnection that unites and divides the characters. It is, after all, what justifies Sir's presence, an articulation of what he forgivingly refers to as "the wishful thinking of lonely people in lonely apartments" (69). Anna's confession crystallizes the play's sense of pervasive emotional desolation, which she alone has the mettle to articulate, difficult as that obviously is. The confessional element itself pervades the play: it is the signature of what Ben calls "our bloody boring reminiscences and our bloody awareness and our bloody quivering sensibilities," all of which make them, in his view, "a close-knit family" (74). Anna, Ben concedes, does not belong, yet she is crucially implicated— largely because she is not obliged to be. She is free to be as she is: "decisive" (60) is one name for her. A "sister" of Sarah in *The Gentle Island,* she is, not surprisingly, the character for whom Sir seems actually to care, and the character who offers him the most provocative challenge.

Her confessional gifts ultimately render irrelevant Father Tom Carty, the friend of the family whose priestly office, ordinarily so central to the ethos of what Miriam refers to as "pure Ballybeg" (25), is disallowed by Sir, relegating the good Father to helplessness.[22] But the removal of the Church's framework does not abolish all sense of structure. Hence the presence of Sir: since he does not exist, it has been necessary to invent him. He is the articulation of the characters' inescapable moral destiny—their remorse, their frailty, their hopeless and poignant desire that things be different.

To emphasize still further the play's dynamics of repetition, freedom, and constraint, Friel subtitles it *After Hippolytus,* as though the playwright himself, about his own official business, is enclosed by identical dynamics. Clearly, the play's plot, with its focus on the disastrous liaison between a stepson and stepmother, is indebted to Euripides, even as it inverts the original's denouement. Once again, however, Friel's focus is not so much on the plot as on the plot's implications, the human image that art contrives to promote. Anna, like Sarah in *The Gentle Island,* has to find some way of maintaining her integrity while ensuring her emotional survival. She does so by means Sarah can only dream of, as Sir relates: "Mrs. Butler, Anna, emigrated to America. . . . She shares an apartment with an English girl. . . . She has never returned to Ireland" (94). She has, without apology, made good the flight prefigured in *Philadelphia, Here I Come!* She seems to live without the Butlers' oppressive structures, as though she has no past, as though silence could be an expression of deliverance. Anna is Sir's opposite; a fiction of potential rather than one of circumscription.

Aristocrats

If *Living Quarters* enacts the finality of aftermath, Friel's next play, *Aristocrats,* first produced at the Abbey Theatre, Dublin, on 8 March 1979, is conceived around the tentativeness of prelude. The Butler family cannot escape the past and are doomed to endless reruns of it. The O'Donnell family in *Aristocrats* is fortuitously freed into a future that catches them somewhat unawares but nevertheless willing to make a go of it.

Once again, the setting is a family reunion: the O'Donnells have reunited for the wedding of the youngest sister, Claire. Returning to join Claire and her sister Judith are their brother Casimir, who lives in Hamburg, and their sister Alice, who lives in London with her husband, Eamon, a native of the nearby village of Ballybeg. Claire, musical and sensitive, is about to enter a quite unsuitable marriage. Judith shoulders virtually all the responsibility of maintaining the decrepit but historic family home, Ballybeg Hall, and the no less important and dilapidated head of the family, senile, bedridden "Father," District Justice O'Donnell (retired).

A local man, Willie Diver, helps Judith, and the household is completed by two other characters. One is an American professor, Tom Hoffnung, researching the history of the Irish Catholic aristocracy, of which previous

O'Donnells were illustrious members. He never tires of asking questions. The other is Uncle George, who doesn't speak until well on into the third act. When he does, it is another manifestation of the unexpected freedom that has befallen the family.

While it is true to say that *Aristocrats* "seems Friel's most Chekhovian job of character drawing,"[23] this view overlooks the way the family's historical and cultural legacy can ensnare its members in useless images of themselves. Casimir is the character of whom that seems to be most true, and Eamon is the character who, in the role of the conscious, critical outsider, is least susceptible to having his sense of reality defined by what the house symbolizes. But these two characters at least are in a position to live out, in the light of their temperaments, the conflicting meanings that the house suggests to them. Tom Hoffnung, on the other hand, perceives the house as a specimen— much as George, in *Volunteers,* regards his precious jug. Hoffnung's name may be translated literally as "hope," but his "digging"[24] is a variety of inter-ment—again, in contrast to the labor of restoration in *Volunteers.* As Eamon tells Casimir: "There are certain things, certain truths . . . that are beyond Tom's kind of scrutiny" (69).

Yet the play does not deny the pleasure Casimir derives from exhibiting such family treasures as the chair in which Gerard Manley Hopkins used to sit, the poet being only one of many famous houseguests to grace Ballybeg Hall in the good old days. Casimir's difficulty with Hoffnung's direct questions, however, are an early indication that he is more concerned with fabricating a glowing past for himself than with providing accurate historical data, a disposition to which Hoffnung is blind. And Casimir's apparently total recall of family history does not include the ability to remember boyhood escapades with Willie Diver, when the latter reminds him of them. Nor does his sense of family pride prevent him from being traumatized by the sound of his father's voice.

Casimir is a pivotal character in the play because of the imaginative and playful elements he objectively represents—in addition to his relationship to his birthplace, there is the pleasure he takes in music (particularly Claire's piano playing) and his invention of the wonderful fantasy croquet game—which are also the source of self-deception. Eamon, predictably, finds a phrase to denote Casimir's complex duality, which he applies to his brother-in-law's present life in Germany (though Eamon is quick to accept the phrase's applicability to himself): "It has the authentic ring of phony fiction" (36). Everybody is susceptible to an image of themselves that, if accepted, both limits and facilitates negotiations between self and world. One such image is "aristocrat," to which Casimir cravenly but enthusiastically aspires. The play, however, shows aristocracy in transition to a less certain, more fluid future.

Such a release is possible, in terms of the play's plot, by the death of the old district justice, whose fatal attack has been brought on by the sound of his daughter Anna's tape-recorded voice. As in the short story "Foundry House" on which this scene draws, the exiled daughter's greetings communicate a tissue of misperceptions about the state of the family. The effect of Father's demise is to show that there is no basis now for keeping up a plausible aristocratic front. Loss of face may result in gain of self. And in any case, the cracks in the front did not appear because the old man died: they were there at the outset—from, for example, Alice's entrance with a black eye coinciding with one of Casimir's particularly fanciful invocations of the past. The family had reunited in order to sanction a supposedly integrative, but in fact nullifying, ritual: Claire's marriage (nullifying because her husband-to-be is a greengrocer with "a great white lorry with an enormous plastic banana on top of the cab"[27]) confirms the decline in social status begun by Alice's marriage to Eamon. It finds itself, instead, attending a supposedly disintegrative, but in fact liberating, ritual: Father's burial.

Each of the characters has a history at odds with the stifling carapace of the past that Ballybeg Hall imposes. Alice drinks. Eamon is fired from a promising diplomatic career for becoming involved with what's loosely called "the movement" (30). Judith has had an illegitimate child; the child lives in an orphanage. Claire thinks of herself as "in a mess" (50), unfit for marriage, and has had a promising career as a musician stymied by Father—as Casimir concedes: "I'm afraid he was adept at stifling things" (66). Casimir should know; having failed as heir apparent to the family's tradition of eminence in the legal profession, he holds some nebulous position in the German sausage industry. Yet it is from the substance of their frailties that they must now make their lives, since they no longer have the social structure of aristocracy to provide them with a defining context. This is the juncture, perhaps, at which the spirit of "plebeian past times. . . . before we were educated out of our emotions" (47) might be resuscitated.

Eamon is the play's embodiment of that spirit. He is the one who breaks defining, image-laden barriers. He marries into the O'Donnell family. He breaks diplomatic ranks. He tenderly attends to emotionally frail Claire and revisits his past emotional attachment to Judith. He hopes that he and Alice have "a context" (84), is entirely committed to his work as Probation Officer, and insists on Uncle George coming to London to live. He reveals to Tom Hoffnung the identity of Father's wife, an actress whose marriage was repressive incarceration. Eamon denounces the O'Donnell aristocratic lineage for "existing only in its own concept of itself" (53). The freedom of such unrelatedness is a freedom not worth having. It eventually undermines itself, as recent family history confirms. Eamon offers as an alternative a web of connectedness and common concern, a way of being conceived of in terms of interdependence and mutuality. He leads them in a valedictory, sentimental song, "Sweet Alice, Ben Bolt," shortly after his use of the phrase in family code for a splendid good time, "a party in Vienna" (84).

The play is careful not to make Eamon too obviously the opposite number of Sir in *Living Quarters,* liberating where Sir constrains, exemplifying rather than directing. In view of his superior awareness of the symbolic and psychological reality of Ballybeg Hall, and in view of his acceptance of the role of cultural conscience in the play, it may come as a surprise that he has a moment of wishing "somehow we'll keep it [the house] going" (77), and that perhaps he doesn't altogether agree with Alice's expression of her feelings: "I don't know what I feel. Maybe a sense of release; of not being pursued; of the possibility of—*(short pause)*—of 'fulfillment'. No. Just emptiness. Perhaps maybe a new start" (83–84).

Yet Eamon's sense of "difficulty" (83), in making him less than totally consistent, humanizes him. It makes him less than a mouthpiece for those values required to lift the play beyond being a portrait of a twilight. It acknowledges the attachment his own family, as servants, had to the aristocracy, a heritage of dependence no less defining than that which he implies the surviving O'Donnells should shed. He too is obliged to practice what he preaches, hence the legitimacy of his exemplary influence. There is nothing prescriptive about Eamon, for all his didactic attacks on Tom Hoffnung. He makes these, he says, because he is "nervous that all you'll see is . . . the make-believe. . . . I'm nervous of us; we don't pose to our best advantage" (55).

Eamon's faith in a reality beneath the "phony fiction" is a liberating influence within the play. That reality cannot be lived within the context of Ballybeg Hall. Yet Eamon needs the help of Judith's hardheaded assessment of the economics of maintaining the house to enable him finally to let go. To start afresh is the play's greatest challenge, and the promise, however tentative, that it is possible to do so is the important cultural message of *Aristocrats.* If there is an aristocracy, the play seems to say, let it be of the spirit: "the imagination is the only conscience."[25] The tentative stalking of the imagination feeling its way that the "Sporadic Diary" recounts is reproduced in the fluid grace of the play's movements, which with their musical accompaniment make *Aristocrats* Friel's most lyrical play.

Friel's Theater of Language

Each great Irish dramatist—Richard Brinsley Sheridan, Oscar Wilde, George Bernard Shaw, J. M. Synge, Samuel Beckett—has in his own way made his name primarily, if not exclusively, on his creation of verbal theater—a form of play, that is, in which what is said, or unsaid, tends to be more important than what is done. In drawing renewed attention to this frequently noted characteristic of Irish drama, the critic Richard Kearney includes Friel among the Irish playwrights for whom it is the case, noting that "Brian Friel's plays in the eighties have become increasingly concerned with the problem of language. So much so that they constitute not just a theatre of language but a theatre *about* language. Words have become both the form *and* the content of his dramas."[26]

This development hardly comes as a surprise, given Friel's preoccupation from the beginning of his career on the contending claims of different tonalities, different discourses, even different accents—Cass McGuire's broad New York accent articulates more than her long residence in that city, it is a brave, energetic articulation of her being a misfit at home; one way of describing Columba's divided loyalties in *The Enemy Within* is to note how he desires to supplant the language of local Irish politics with that of prayer; Gar O'Donnell's expert mimicry attempts to offset the tension of the potential birth of a real, inimitable self in Philadelphia.

The plays following *Aristocrats* install language as a central dramatizing agent. The contradictions in narrative and memory found in the depositions of *Faith Healer* not only act as reminders of what fragile resources narration and reminiscing are, they also enact, at an exclusively verbal level, incompatibilities and dependencies that are at the heart of the play's vision of human frailty. In *Translations* historical process is the source of contradiction. Here, frailty resides in culture and habitat, a frailty dramatized by the vulnerability of the language that gives culture and habitat distinctive identities. The virtual silencing of the Irish language in the nineteenth century, a complex and inconclusive series of events with the onset of which *Translations* deals, is taken as a means of exploring questions of perennial interest concerning relations between cultures, the relevance of minorities, and the interconnections between place and personality. But the pieties honored in *Translations* are satirized in *The Communication Cord,* where responsibility for linguistic duplicity and cultural misprision is located within individuals rather than in social, political, or historical agencies. And as though to confirm the central place of language in his artistic thought, Friel turns to translation and adaptation in *Three Sisters* and *Fathers and Sons.*

The Russian plays are significant not merely by being translations, however. They too extend and diversify the themes of their predecessors, with their elaborate yet intimate rehearsals of word giving, promising, and associated variations on interpersonal discourse. Here again the elusiveness and apparent temporariness of language—aspects of the word that the dramatic enterprise as a whole implicitly ratifies—are much to the fore. In *Three Sisters* and *Fathers and Sons*, however, there seems more tolerance of language's duplicity. The only character to use language consistently in *Three Sisters* is Solyony, and his consistency is murderous: Tusenbach's death is the outcome of Solyony's earlier promise to kill any rival to his misdirected claim on Irina. Bazarov, in *Fathers and Sons*, aims for verbal consistency, and is both humanized and victimized by his inability to overcome its inconsistency.

These Russian plays also seem to complete Friel's dismantling of Ballybeg. The untenability of the place as a family locale—as a place that existed primarily to be forsaken—is fully faced in *Living Quarters* and *Aristocrats*, where the treatment of Ballybeg acts as an illuminating reprise of a theme from *Philadelphia*. In *Faith Healer, Translations*, and *The Communication Cord*, Ballybeg is presented as a cultural terminus, a place where certain forms of public life—the faith healer's performance, the hedge school in *Translations*, exploitative sentimentality regarding the past in *The Communication Cord*—come to crises from which they cannot recover, crises which are explicitly connected with the power, adequacy, and dependability of language. Nowhere does the statement by Manus Sweeney in *The Gentle Island* that "every story has seven faces" seem more true than in Friel's later plays.

Faith Healer

Eamon in *Aristocrats*, for all the power of his example, is no miracle worker. It is precisely to such a figure, however, that Friel turns in his next play, *Faith Healer*, first produced at the Longacre Theater, New York, on 5 April 1979, with the celebrated English actor James Mason playing faith healer Frank Hardy.

Faith Healer "may well be the finest play to come out of Ireland since J. M. Synge's *Playboy of the Western World* . . . a work of profound and scintillating originality."[27] One reason for this judgment is the play's form: it "attempts one of the most difficult of all dramatic tasks, the unfolding of a story entirely by monologues."[28] Between opening and closing monologues from Frank Hardy, the faith healer, come those by his wife, Grace, and his manager, Teddy. Once again Friel has created a different kind of play, dealing with material that ostensibly owes little to its predecessors, and presenting his audience with a completely new set of challenges. Yet despite its innovative character, *Faith Healer* is a further clarification of very well-established themes. When the play opens, the two main characters, Frank Hardy and his wife Grace, have died, leaving the manager of the traveling faith-healing show, Teddy, as the only character to address the audience "in reality." The last phrase requires quotation marks to draw attention to its dubious, shifting status in the play. Virtually every circumstance in the play is subject to different interpretations. There is no agreement as to Frank's origins, the legal status of his marriage to Grace, or the weather during the sojourn in Scotland (one of the play's three climactic events). Even the fact that Frank and Grace are dead from the start does not emerge at once, as a similar circumstance does in *The Freedom of the City*. Everything is open to question, to revision, to doubt.

This state of flux applies even, or perhaps especially, to the healing faith for which Frank is a conduit: he finds it impossible to take it on trust: "Was it all chance?—or skill?—or illusion?—or delusion? Precisely what power did I possess? . . . Did it reside in my ability to invest someone with faith in me or did I evoke from him a healing faith in himself? . . . You're beginning to masquerade, aren't you? You're becoming a husk, aren't you? And so it went on and on and on. Silly, wasn't it? . . . But they persisted right to the end, those nagging, tormenting, maddening questions that rotted my life."[29] Frank cannot abide by the faith he enacts, cannot reconcile its authority with a sense of his own authenticity.

But Frank is nothing without his questions. He is an instrument of faith, empowered and stigmatized by his gift, different from his fellow man. Yet by his questions and his fabrications he reveals a human resistance to the unearthly ability with which he has been fated. But, as the very prosody of Frank's questioning reveals, the wholeness that the collaboration and mutuality between faith and healing presupposes escapes him.

The play is based on memory, and all three characters are implicitly free to recollect as their consciousnesses dictate. This freedom is implied by the monologue. In this form, the presence of another character obviously does not impinge; there is no danger of being overheard; there is no need to conform to the expectations of a susceptible auditor. These features are brought out in the rambling character of the play's four addresses. Despite being verbally and physically detached from each other, the characters are indissolubly connected on the basis of three crucial events in which they were jointly, although not to equal degrees, involved.

These events, which may be regarded as the three acts that constitute the drama of Frank Hardy, are his healing ten Welsh country folk in a single evening; the stillbirth of Grace's child in Kinlochbervie in the north of Scotland; and Frank's murder in Ballybeg by some country folk he fails to cure. None of these events occurs on stage. Since the play gives priority to retrospection, commentary, questioning, and evaluation, there is only the characters' word for them. Nevertheless, none of the three deny that those events took place. The events, in a sense, possess a collective, impersonal truth, which individual recollection of them distorts.

Events are complete and have an ineffaceable, enduring influence. Reactions are partial and subject to change. Events transpire, the products of invisible agencies and forces that in the play go under the code words "faith" (the healing), "nature" (the birth) and "evil" (the murder). The abstract character of those terms emphasizes the invisibility and inscrutability of their true meaning. Consciousness pants in pursuit of these meanings, always belated, always deceived, always frustrated. *Faith Healer* makes the panting audible by revealing how it is the outcome of the *danse macabre* between two impossible yet inseparable partners. Events have the force of destiny. Grace speaks of Frank's "feud between himself and his talent" (25).

Grace also sees Frank engrossed by the total event of faith healing: "always before a performance he'd be . . . in complete mastery—yes, that's close to it—in such complete mastery that everything is harmonized for him, in such mastery that anything is possible. . . . And then, for him, I didn't exist" (20–21). There seems to be a relationship between such completeness and the stillbirth, which is spoken of as "a finished thing" (21). And the terms in which Frank faces his murderers seem to belong to the same vocabulary of definitiveness and completeness:

And as I walked I became possessed of a strange and trembling intimation: that the whole corporeal world—the cobbles, the trees, the sky . . . somehow they had shed their physical reality and had become mere imaginings, and that in all existence there was only myself and the wedding guests. And that intimation in turn gave way to a stronger sense: that even we had ceased to be physical and existed only in spirit, only in the need we had for each other. . . . And as I moved across that yard towards them and offered myself to them, then for the first time I had a simple and genuine sense of home-coming. Then, for the first time there was no atrophying terror; and the maddening questions were silent. (44)

The need of which Frank speaks here is what Grace represents, the saving grace, as it were, by which faith can be upheld. Emotionally deprived by a stern Ulster father, Grace does not possess Frank's powers of transformation, and thus is a constant reminder to him of the fragility and accidental nature of the merely human. It is this nature he brutalizes, seeks to escape through drink and through denial, not because he cannot face it (his faith-healing ministrations obviously require him to do exactly that), but because he cannot stand the thought of it. It is the objective embodiment of his own misgivings about the value of life and the value of his own erratically redemptive commitment. It is what resists his questions. Teddy, whose description of the Kinlochbervie episode is the fullest, recounts that Frank did not abandon Grace in her great hour of need because of callousness or ignorance. He did so "because he had suffered all that she had suffered"; without denying that walking away was "bloody-minded of him," Teddy goes on, "maybe being the kind of man he was, you know, with that strange gift he had, I've thought maybe—well, maybe he had to have his own way of facing things" (36).

Teddy also believes that Frank could be "never anything more than a mediocre artist" (30–31), because "his bloody brains has him bloody castrated" (31). Grace's mention of "performance" and Teddy's of "artist" reveal another aspect of *Faith Healer:* "we have here a complex metaphor of the artist who is possessed by a gift over which he has no control."[30] Indeed, *Faith Healer* might be considered a condensed and more intense version of *Crystal and Fox.* It has the earlier play's destructive protagonist; Grace is another Crystal in her thankless but crucial role as an embodiment of emotional need; both plays have for their immediate backdrop a traveling show; Frank's last words, "At long last I was renouncing chance" (44), are the ones Fox comes very close to uttering. Obviously the intellectual content of *Faith Healer* is more to the fore than it was in *Crystal and Fox,* and Friel's presentation of it is verbally and dramaturgically more complex. *Faith Healer* also recalls another Friel play, *Living Quarters,* with its emphasis on being trapped in recollection and emotional deprivation. And is the spirit of what Eamon in *Aristocrats* seeks to provide suggested by Frank's description of himself as "an aristocrat" (12) when his performances go well?

The relationships in *Faith Healer* between thought and action, between word and deed, between chaos and form, between creation and destruction are all germane to an artist's work. Faith healing itself seems an apt and moving metaphor for the artist's role, with its alleviating and restorative connotations, and the implication that art is nature's necessary complement. And there is an age-old tissue of associations between the magical, the hieratic, and the artistic upon which the character of Frank tacitly draws. Such associations, indeed, originate with the earliest manifestations of theater, in which connections between ritual, sacrifice, exalted words, and the force of destiny are very much to the fore. The ritual of faith healing has several obvious theatrical features, including the role-playing confidence of the healer and the malleability and suggestibility of his audience.

Yet, appealing and plausible as *Faith Healer's* metaphorical dimension is, the play ultimately does not endorse it. The metaphor of Frank as artist does not account for his destructiveness. It cannot justify or explain his treatment of Grace, which is clearly the opposite of the redemptive, enhancing influence symbolized by his gift. Grace, who has nothing but her life to give, who exists in a state of nature rather than a state of faith, doubt, or both, persists until she has nothing left. When Frank is killed, Grace loses the pretext for and object of those human qualities, such as loyalty, love, and physical commitment, that are more familiar, more comprehensible expressions of faith than anything demonstrated by Frank's gift. Without Frank, Grace kills herself.

This seemingly melodramatic outcome occurs not for the sake of effect, but as a reminder of the reciprocal nature of what the two characters embody, the mutuality and dissonance of their different forms of faith and their different ways of healing. In perhaps his most sophisticated use of the familiar divided character, Friel shows Frank and Grace divided against each other and, as an apparently necessary consequence, each divided in him- or herself. By their separate natures they are forever alienated from, and forever implicated in, the otherness they cannot embody. As Teddy puts it: "And what was the fighting all about in the end? All right, you could say it was because the only thing that finally mattered to him was his work—and that would be true. Or you could say it was because the only thing that finally mattered to her was him—and I suppose that would be true too. But when you put the two propositions together like that—I don't know—somehow they both become only half-truths, you know" (33).

In which case, the complementary half of the truth the play as a whole contains is Teddy himself. The shocking deaths of Frank and Grace— needless, inevitable, and self-willed as they are, the result of an undifferentiated interaction of creative and anticreative powers, of a hapless marriage between art and nature—overshadow the fact of Teddy's survival. His survival is notably undramatic. He possesses an inscrutable ability to accept whatever he has witnessed. He does not strain at the bounds of his world, yet is a technician vital to Frank's performances. He is the one character who is permitted to observe, "you've got to be a realist . . . live in the present" (36), and whose fate it is to do just that, the very thing that is so difficult for Frank and Grace.

The slight sense of strain in his "you've got to" suggests that he is aware of there being a choice and that he has made his choice by keeping his eye closely fixed on what is in front of them from moment to moment—though this does not mean he is unaffected by another's pain, as his reaction to Grace's suicide graphically reveals. Teddy's is the longest single monologue, largely because of its profuse detail, a profusion that emphasizes his endurance through time.

If Frank and Grace are all passionate involvement and extravagant emotion, Teddy is the stoical, detached alternative. He is unaware of having a fate; Frank and Grace cannot escape awareness of theirs. Frank is the incurable performer; Teddy is the eternal assistant stage manager. Grace awaits anxiously in the wings; Teddy sits disinterestedly in the audience. Frank and Grace are social outsiders; yet Teddy's lowbrow sympathies, his neo-Dickensian characteristics (which make him endearing and a little sad), seem to make him, in his ordinariness, an outsider also. If there is more to life than theatrical anecdotes, animal acts, and "a professional relationship" (39)—and Frank and Grace surely confirm that there is—Teddy is immune to it. But *Faith Healer* does not enjoin that Teddy be preferred over Frank and Grace, or vice versa; to contemplate their separate and collective presences is drama enough. By including Teddy, however, it attains as a text a completeness of which each of its characters' lives is deprived. Drawing on the parable-making side of Friel's imagination, *Faith Healer* is his most condensed, inexhaustible, intense treatment of his long-standing existential preoccupations.

Translations

Friel's next play has come to be regarded as his most important and was perceived from the first to have numerous significant cultural resonances. Some of these resonances may be detected in the fact that *Translations* was the inaugural production of the Field Day Theatre Company, and that its premiere took place at the Guildhall, Derry, on 23 September 1980—less than ten years after *The Freedom of the City* availed of the same building for quite other symbolic purposes. The response of the London *Times* reviewer gives a general sense of how the play has been received since its opening night: "I have never been more certain of witnessing the premiere of a national classic."[31] Subsequent successful productions in London and New York, together with the conferring of the Ewart-Biggs Memorial Award for Anglo-Irish understanding in 1981, have confirmed the play's importance and popularity and have established its position as "a culmination in [Friel's] dramatic career"[32]—though it is not *the* culmination.

Translations is set, as the note in the text says, "in a hedge-school in the townland of Baile Beag/Ballybeg, an Irish-speaking community in County Donegal." The time of the action is "late August, 1833".[33] Some of the play's cultural implications will be better appreciated if these details are enlarged. Hedge schools were the informal places of learning the Irish peasantry attended, being disqualified on the grounds of religion and property from attending more formal establishments. The name is a literal description of these sites of learning in their early days during the eighteenth century. In the words of one authority on the subject: "Because the law forbade the schoolmaster to teach, he was compelled to give instruction secretly: because the house-holder was penalised for harbouring the schoolmaster, he had perforce to teach, and that only when the weather permitted, out of doors. He therefore selected, in some remote spot, the sunny side of a hedge or bank which effectively hid him and his pupils from the eye of a chance passer-by. . . . Later when the laws against education were less strictly enforced, school was taught in a cabin, a barn, or any building that might be given or lent for the purpose, but the name 'Hedge School' was still retained."[34] Thus in *Translations* class is held "in a disused barn or hay-shed or byre" (11); this is also home for the schoolmaster, Hugh Mor O'Donnell, and his son Manus.

The play opens with Manus teaching Sarah, a young peasant girl, to say her name, a vignette that rehearses some of the play's major themes, as well as having an influential bearing on the plot. The relevance of what Manus is doing can be seen immediately by contrasting Sarah with the other peasant present, sixty-year-old Jimmy, "the Infant Prodigy," whose intimate acquaintance with Homer, Virgil, and Ovid has kept him in a state of innocence and isolation from the ways of the world. Manus believes that with speech Sarah can do more in the world than Jimmy. Her act of translating silence into speech is implicitly more significant than Jimmy's translations of Latin and Greek, as Manus's words of encouragement suggest: "Nothing will stop us now! Nothing in the wide world!" (12). The naiveté of this enthusiasm returns to haunt him later in the play.

The main business of the first act is a depiction of the hedge school in action as the young adult students arrive for class after their day's work in the field. Such a scene, with its vitality and commitment, does as much as anything in modern Irish theater to erase the stereotype of the Irish peasant— drunken, fighting, cohabiting with pigs, craven, superstitious. This stereotype was particularly current in the nineteenth century.[35] Friel believes that his peasants have minds and that they are alive to learning.

Yet the school is not as secure an establishment as it might seem. Mention is made of the soldiers present in the townland to map the area for the Ordnance Survey Commission. The "sweet smell" (21) of potato blight is in the air. Maire, Manus's sweetheart, wants a material confirmation of the security that their love represents, and since he is reluctant to seek it, she is busy making plans to go to America; hence she is eager to learn English. Her desire to do so, for which she cites the authority of Daniel O'Connell, the foremost Irish politician of the day and the most successful Irish Catholic constitutional politician in history, alerts the audiences to a witty dramatic device, namely that though the audience understands the actors to be speaking English, it should also understand that the characters are actually speaking Irish. As for Manus, the main source of Maire's impatience with him is his unwillingness to compete for the position of principal of the new National School (an institution of primary education, established by the British government in conformity with its educational policies and cultural objectives). In a word, then, Ballybeg is beset by change.

The Ordnance Survey has met with some resistance, presumably because it is being carried out by troops.[36] As described by Doalty, one of the students, the resistance has a strain of practical joking in it, though it is clear that when he mentions the Donnelly twins something more sinister is implied. Maire objects to Doalty's japes; Manus defends them as "a gesture. . . . Just to indicate a presence" (18).[37] The apparent compatibility, however, of what Manus calls "a bloody military operation" (32) with the establishment of a local National School is not questioned. Hugh O'Donnell, the hedge school master, considers himself a pedagogue for all seasons and contexts. There is no conception in his mind of the cultural cost of supplanting the hedge school. The play articulates the nature of that cost by placing the O'Donnell family where their world's contending cultural forces intersect, although any chance they might have of recognizing that critical position is blurred, because it is one of their own—Owen, Manus's brother—who places them in it.

Owen's arrival in the company of two of the military surveyors, Captain Lancey and Lieutenant Yolland, seems to add to the play's opening mood of bonhomie. His presence in such company is not remarked upon, nor is his employment by them in the role of translator. He seems to be successful in the world beyond Ballybeg. Owen, in his turn, expresses delight at his generous welcome by exclaiming, with equal good nature and blindness: "I come back after six years and everything's just as it was!" (27). But he is known as Roland to the military; he ignores the fact that Sarah is able to greet him; and he introduces Maire to Yolland as though she and Manus are not to be thought of together—as indeed they may not be, since the rift in the relationship seems to be widening, and they cannot find the circumstances in which to talk about it. (But Owen knows nothing of this.)

For all his worldly experience and citified dress, and for all that he confides in Yolland that he "got out in time" (37)—out of the family, that is, and hence considers himself better off than Manus—he is unable to face Manus's questioning of his status as a man of two worlds:

MANUS: And they call you Roland!

OWEN: Shhhhh. Isn't it ridiculous? . . .

MANUS: Aren't you going to tell them?

OWEN: Yes—yes—soon—soon.

MANUS: But they . . .

OWEN: Easy, man, easy. Owen—Roland—what the hell. It's only a name. It's the same me, isn't it?

MANUS: Indeed it is. It's the same Owen.

OWEN: And the same Manus. And in a way we complement each other. (33)

But Owen is not willing to take responsibility for what their complementarity might mean.

His assumption that reality exists independently of the language that names it also has a significance that Owen does not confront. His job as translator requires them to find English-language equivalents for Irish place-names. He does his work as though it is a narrow lexical exercise. It is not that he is ignorant of the cultural associations that the changes inevitably muffle, as his lecture on the onomastics of Tobair Vree (43–44) bears out; it is, rather, that like everyone else in Ballybeg, Owen cannot connect change to its consequences.[38]

Clearly, the townland will still contain its familiar hills and streams, however they are named. In that sense, it is easy to understand why Owen considers names irrelevant. He has not perceived, however, another irrelevance— that of changing names in order to carry out a geographical survey. There is no necessary connection between the theodolite and the dictionary. The fact that it has been deemed necessary by the powers that be to change place-names defines the arbitrary but incontrovertible character of those powers. Such power is hardly being deployed whimsically. The changes of name mean that the places renamed can now be spoken of in a different language than that used by those who live in those places. Linguistic differences are not merely phonological, etymological, or lexical. Language does not merely exist as a self-contained linguistic enterprise. It exists, rather more familiarly, as a network of cultural encodings, a tissue of interrelated namings and of cognitive assumptions made on the basis of acquaintance with those names. To change names, thus, is to replace those assumptions and, in the case in point, to speak of the townland of Ballybeg not merely in terms of hill and stream but in terms of control, such as *law, property, taxation,* and the like. The cultural expropriation codifies and ratifies those earlier forms of expropriation, one of whose effects was to bring hedge schools into being. This is how the play translates Captain Lancey's statement that "the present survey has for its object the relief which can be afforded to the proprietors and occupiers of land from unequal taxation" (31), though Owen's rough translation of this and the rest of what Lancey says is made with a casualness that suggests that he is indifferent to the survey's ultimate meaning or that he simply has a general sense of Lancey's words and cannot fully comprehend their applicability to a world that he has just discovered to be, apparently, proof against change.

Owen's companion is the dreamy Yolland, with whom his anglicized name (Roland) forms a half-rhyme, just as slow Manus is partnered with hasty Maire and Hugh with self-deluded Jimmy. Yolland considers Ireland "Eden," and has fallen for his new surroundings in terms that recall Frank Hardy's fateful surrender to Ballybeg—coming to Ireland begets "a curious sensation. . . . It was a momentary sense of discovery; no—not quite a sense of discovery—a sense of recognition, of confirmation of something I half knew instinctively. . . . I had moved into a consciousness that wasn't striving nor agitated, but at its ease and with its own conviction and assurance" (40). Such romanticism comes to fruition when, through Owen's good offices, Yolland attends a dance at Maire's house, and she and the lieutenant fall for each other, conducting a poignant, tender love scene that culminates in a kiss. But Sarah sees the kiss and reports it to Manus. And Yolland is never seen alive again.

From the impossible union between Maire and Yolland things fall apart in the play. Manus leaves home, not to take the job of schoolmaster he's been offered in one of the neighbouring islands, but to disappear into the hinterland. Sarah, to whom Manus gave speech, is struck dumb when peremptorily asked to identify herself by Captain Lancey. Maire is desolate and attempts to reconstruct a sense of who Yolland is by reciting the names of the Norfolk villages that make up his part of the world, names which to her are "strange sounds. . . . But nice sounds; like Jimmy Jack reading his Homer" (60). Meanwhile, threats are issued and carried out by Captain Lancey as to the fate of Ballybeg if Yolland is not found, the severity of which prompt Owen to recognise that his activities have been "all a mistake" (66). His response to this admission is to try to make contact with the nefarious Donnelly twins. All of this bears out Manus's view that the survey is "a bloody military operation," though its attempts to turn to violent account what has been lost in translation between Maire and Yolland shows how imitable the tactics of the Donnelly twins prove to be and how, given the power, even the passionate, intimate encounter between two strangers can be adapted to policy considerations.

Finally the stage is left to Hugh and Jimmy, the two characters in the play who for all their verbal sensitivity and etymological interest in translation have the least active or effective contact with their immediate world. In Jimmy's case, this lack of involvement leaves him free to envisage with glee his impending marriage to Pallas Athena. In Hugh's case, it leads to a symbolic embodiment of the play's historical argument.

If language has power, Hugh is the one who should wield it. He is the character who seems to recognize most clearly the changes that are taking place around him. It is he who, reflecting that "we must learn those new names. . . . We must learn to make them our own. We must make them our new home" (66), also offers a means of retaining what is in danger of being lost: "it is not the literal past, the 'facts' of history, that shape us, but images of the past embodied in language" (66). It is Hugh also who describes Ballybeg's cultural vulnerability: "it can happen that a civilisation can be imprisoned in a linguistic contour which no longer matches the landscape of . . . fact" (43).

Yet all he possesses is this histrionic or, to use Owen's word, "pompous" (43) language. His application for the headship of the new National School, which he was confident would be successful, fails. Accustomed to the role of father of his people, he is left at the end with no people. His sons are on the run, and the larger, communal family of the hedge school is dispersed and on the defensive. Like Manus Sweeney in *The Gentle Island,* Hugh is "king of nothing." In this condition, Maire comes to ask him for English lessons and for the translation of the one word of English which she retains from her evening with Yolland, "always." Hugh responds: "*Semper—per omnia saecula.* The Greeks call it '*aei*.' It's a silly word" (67).

If it is, history has made it so. And if Hugh believes that the Irish "like to think we endure around truths immemorially posited" (42), by the end of the play it is hard for him to find a place where such truths dwell. Hence his acknowledgment of the change that has befallen Ballybeg comes from the citation and translation of a classical precedent. This translation closes the play, and with it Hugh personifies both continuity and the detachment required to ensure that, in his own words, "confusion is not an ignoble condition" (67). If "the real subject of the play is the relation between authority and alienation,"[39] Hugh is a potent symbol of it. Poised between past and present, between tradition and change, between silence and instruction, Hugh embodies in unresolved, and thus explicit, form the interlocking tensions of Friel's most ambitious play. His final speech, citing Virgil's *Aeneid*, itself an extraordinary work of cultural appropriation and "translation" of Homer's *Odyssey*, is intended to defend, by means of language's grandeur, against the changes that have befallen Ballybeg and the hedge school that was its community focus.[40] Unwittingly, however, it movingly underlines them, revealing Hugh himself to be "imprisoned in a linguistic contour." If the play is faithful to Friel's intention that it eschew politics and "concern itself only with the exploration of the dark and private places of individual souls,"[41] Hugh embodies that fidelity.

The Communication Cord

Field Day first produced Friel's next play, *The Communication Cord,* at the Guildhall, Derry, on 21 September 1982. (An earlier production of his version of Chekhov's *Three Sisters* is discussed in the treatment of Friel's Russian translations at the end of this chapter.)[42]

The Communication Cord deals with the amorous, linguistic, and social adventures of Tim Gallagher, a young, not particularly articulate academic working on a doctoral thesis entitled "Discourse Analysis with Particular Reference to Response Cries."[43] (Response cries are voluntary or involuntary expressions of an emotional nature that occur in the course of conversation: a definitive example is the "O my God" that closes the play.) The site of Tim's adventures is an old, restored peasant's cottage near Ballybeg, County Donegal, property of the McNeilis family, one of whom, Jack, Tim's friend, is a smooth-talking, successful Dublin barrister. They have come to the cottage so that Tim can impress his sweetheart, Susan Donovan, and more importantly, her father, Senator Doctor Donovan, by entertaining them in the cottage. If impressed, the senator doctor may decide to change for the better Tim's untenured status at the University, thus placing him in a sufficiently secure position to marry Susan, which is what Susan wants.

From the outset, then, and throughout the play, language is seen as a means of talking oneself into or out of a given situation. It is understood by the characters to lend credibility and definition to whatever transaction they have in mind. Like the cottage, language is a matter of pastiche rather than a matter of authenticity. As the play develops, however, it becomes clear that material phenomena, not to mention other people, resist the arbitrary control language presumes to impose on them. Thus, not only does the cottage fire afflict Tim with clouds of befogging smoke, but the cottage itself turns out to be already occupied by his colleague and former girlfriend, Claire Harkin. Local residents participate in the proliferating chaos that breaks loose when what Tim describes—speaking academically, but unwittingly previewing the course of the play's events—no longer holds good: "All social behaviour, the entire social order, depends on our communicational structures, on words mutually agreed on and mutually understood" (18).

Appropriately, not even the play's title may be taken literally. Communication as a cord out of which "the net" (19) of inference, implication, and mutuality may be woven—a whole fabric of social interaction, linguistically conceived—is one of the play's particularly potent conceits, all the more incisive in view of the plot's basic orientation around the matter of mutually significant and mutually advantageous personal relationships. But the communication cord is also a mechanism used when a bus or train is out of control or when there is an emergency on board; and certainly the play's farcical alarums and diversions give substance to this other—more familiar, less inventive—meaning of the title. The characters in the play who take their language literally, and who tend to overlook the contributions made to discourse by the nuance of context and the quirk of personality, are those who practice a preemptive rather than an interactive way with the world, with unfortunate consequences for themselves.

To a considerable extent, all the characters suffer these consequences, though to varying degrees (in *The Communication Cord,* Friel's sense of character fluctuation, inconsistency, and variousness reaches its fullest expression). In particular, the play takes aim at the character who has the most prominent social role, Senator Doctor Donovan. And in a typical example of how Friel links public and private attitudes, Donovan's cultured obtuseness finds a counterpart in his gullible, unenlightened attitude toward personal relationships. His view of the cottage, with its unused peasant paraphernalia all intact, moves him to extravagances of nostalgic fervor, which Friel satirically juxtaposes with the repeated criticisms of the place by the play's one Ballybeg native, Nora Dan. His accidental entrapment by the cattle post, ostensibly the cottage's most authentic relic, provides for his crudely comic comeuppance and is another of the play's revealing reminders of the incorrigible difference that remains between words and things.

The senator doctor is a spokesman for typically sentimentalizing attitudes to rural Ireland ("This is the touchstone. That landscape, that sea, this house—this is the apotheosis" [31]), and *The Communication Cord* exposes the shallowness of modern Ireland's citified pseudosophistication. Jack, whose cottage in effect it is, embodies in his glibness and manipulation an ostensible command of the present that is the counterpart of the Senator's cultural credentials.

One of the outcomes of the Senator's attitude is a pious, protective attitude to his daughter Susan, who is well able to look after herself. In Jack's case, there is a reciprocal reification of women; rather than behave protectively to them, he acquires and discards them. This depersonalizing behavior is marked by his application of the same phrase to two entirely different women: "part of me died" (24, 67).

If the Senator is "hypocrisy incarnate, a symbol of the very *discontinuity* in Irish cultural history which he refuses to acknowledge,"[44] Jack seems to embody a knowing indifference to the past. In his case, the cottage, with its bare central room, is a space to be filled by "roles," as Tim notes (19), that Jack casts.

Tim, while central to the action, lacks the definition of Jack and the senator. While these two frame the context of the play's discourse, Tim provides the unrehearsable "response." His partner, therefore, is Claire—not because she also supplies the responses but because she subverts the Jack-inspired designs, which Tim believes it is in his best interest to obey. Claire does this both by allowing herself to be cast in the role of Evette (a cliché French sexbomb, shared unknowingly by Jack and the Senator) and by refusing to comply with that role. Her erratic course throughout the play, wordlessly dropping compromising objects (articles of intimate feminine attire, in the best theatrical tradition of farce) in Tim's putative path to emotional and professional security, is a splendidly individualized and fully self-conscious piece of acting out.

As with Jack and the Senator, where consciousness and unconsciousness form a culturally manipulative twosome, so too with Claire and Tim. In both cases, the unit formed is a more potent and more articulate entity than the units of discourse that Tim keeps talking about as fundamental to the enterprise of human exchange. In order to demonstrate the power articulated by the combination of naive Tim and playful Claire, they enter with their play-ending kiss into a pre- or perhaps subverbal world, the kiss an emblem of that naturalness, a tolerance for which is so crucial to Friel's work. Another demonstration of the kiss's power, of course, is that it accidently brings the cottage crashing down. The kiss is more authentic than the too "pat, too 'authentic'" (11) cottage playhouse.

As though to confirm the link between language and culture, the play features several outsiders—the German known as Barney the Banks, Evette, and Nora Dan—each of whom is said to embody the clichés of their cultural origins, and who, despite that, make individualized contributions that clarify the flawed, artificial connections between linguistic usage and cultural status assumed by Jack and the Senator.

Three Sisters

Friel's increasing preoccupation with language as a cultural instrument—discernible in his work from at least *The Freedom of the City* onward—makes it not surprising that he eventually would try his hand at translation. Neither is his choice of texts, Chekhov's *Three Sisters,* surprising. As early in his career as *Philadelphia, Here I Come!,* Chekhovian notes were heard in his work.[45] Perhaps these notes became more audible for his having been present in Minneapolis for Tyrone Guthrie's production of *Three Sisters* (from a translation by Guthrie himself and Leonid Kipnis).[46] More recently, in *Aristocrats* and *Living Quarters,* Friel had centered plays around the fates of three sisters.[47]

Friel has stated: "This translation was undertaken primarily as an act of love and, since the only Chekhov translations available to the Irish theatre are American and English, in the hope that this translation may make the unique experience of Chekhov more accessible to Irish audiences."[48] In other words, the translation is the product of intimate acquaintance with Chekhov's work and of the increasingly explicit interest in language and the manner in which it is necessarily assumed to be an efficient and dependable codification of a mutually shared reality.

Friel's approach has been described as a comparative treatment of various other versions of the play in English: "he simply sat down at his desk with six English versions in front of him."[49] Its emphasis is mainly linguistic, therefore, and the temptation has been resisted to change every feature of the play from a Russian to an Irish context. Thus Irina's birthday gift from Chebyutikin remains the preposterous and unwittingly insulting samovar, and the strong social attachment between the sisters and the military is retained, though it is difficult to imagine the same social relations existing in an Irish context (as the Butler family's claustrophobia and social remoteness in *Living Quarters* confirm).

Friel is careful to ensure, however, that the translation of Chekhov into the English spoken in Ireland is not a mere matter of giving the characters stage-Irish demotic to speak. The character who uses the play's closest approximation to this glib idiom is Natasha, the crassest, least self-aware character in *Three Sisters.* But Natasha is not being handed "black marks and a hundred lines" (to use the idiom of Kulygin) for lines such as those that usher in the company:

OLGA: Ah, Natasha's here. How are you, Natasha?
NATASHA: As my mother used to say, "Never felt better and had less" . . .
          God but that's a wild big crowd, Olga. I could never face that
          crowd. (33)

In Natasha's case such language acts as an anticipation of her pretentious use
of French later on, as well as her forceful use of the language of class hostility
with her servants. The issue is not one of idiom, Irish or otherwise, but of
what use of a specific idiom reveals about a character.

Natasha's Anglo-Irish demotic, with its apparent candor and spontaneity,
gives a sense of Natasha to which she herself declines to subscribe. Her verbal
variety is, as Friel sees it, a counterpart to her emotionally erratic nature. Her
inability to be conscious of her oscillations between various verbal codes (and
the social roles that they imply) acts hand in glove with the mixed signals she
gives as wife and mother. The implied links between being conscious, behaving responsibly towards one's loved ones, and language authenticated by individuality and commitment (language that is one's own because of its
ability to embrace that of another) are links that Natasha cannot maintain.

For Friel, *Three Sisters* is a play about the reality and fragility of such links.
His treatment of the original, or of translations of the original, does not consist, therefore, of grafting idioms familiar to an Irish audience onto the characters' exposition of the plot. It consists, rather, of insinuating an Irish accent
into the proceedings in order to explore and reveal the dramatic relationships
that exist between the characters and such elements of language as idiom, nuance, verbal tic, and silence. Natasha is the play's most blatant case of linguistic disarray and emotional irresponsibility. If *The Communication Cord* has its
characters create false contexts in order either to distort or produce false illusions of consistency, the characters in *Three Sisters* attempt the opposite.
Their painful honesty makes conclusive communication just as problematic,
with the difference that their "response cries" are distressingly moving, and
ultimately unanswerable.

Friel's translation of Chekhov, therefore, is an illuminating and affecting
entrance into a work that has typically been regarded as dealing with society
rather than one about language, a play about the internal exile that can afflict
emotionally deprived people whether they are in Ballybeg or a provincial city
in imperial Russia. The precision of the translation's perception of language
delineates with wonderful clarity the characters' dilemmas, particularly in
those cases where consciousness and unconsciousness of verbal effect coincide. The coincidence is most obviously seen in the male characters—in
Vershinin's mocking and resigned tones, in his gestures of wordless resigna-

tion; in Kulygin's pedantry; in what Friel translates as "quack-quack" by Solyony; and Tusenbach's repetition of "to coin a phrase." The men seem undeceived by their language, whereas the three sisters retain some of their illusions. Moscow is no longer available to them, but being emotionally more resourceful, they implicitly retain a faith in what Moscow symbolizes. Olga's line that closes the play—"If only we knew" (114)—expresses most poignantly the crux of language and action in the play. But it is she and her sisters who have entered most scrupulously into their fate: all the men (except Andrey) are able to leave—the one thing that the sisters wish to do. Thus they combine, in a way that make them members of Friel's theatrical family, the need for illusion and the experience of self-realization, a combination that seems to be the fate particularly of Friel's women. They embody that bittersweet sense of "continuance" first encountered in Friel's short-story "Among the Ruins."

Friel's translation successfully releases what Sir Tyrone Guthrie esteemed in Chekhov: "a current of poetry, expressed by his use of symbols and of leitmotifs, recurrent ideas and phrases associated with certain ideas. . . . These themes expressed, as it were, contrapuntally by different voices and in different contexts, give to his plays the character of chamber music."[50] Friel's recital of Chekhov's music may be heard in counterpoint to the strains of the departing military band:

Just listen to that music. It's so assured, so courageous. It makes you want to go on, doesn't it? Oh my God! Yes, of course we will die and be forgotten—everything about us, how we looked, how we spoke, that there were three of us. But our unhappiness, our suffering, won't be wasted. They're a preliminary to better times, and because of them the people who come after us will inherit a better life—a life of peace and content and happiness. And they will look on us with gratitude and with love. But our life isn't over yet. By no means! We are going to go on living! And that music is so confident, so courageous, it almost seems as if it is about to be revealed very soon why we are alive and what our suffering is for. If only we knew that. If only we knew that. (113–114)

Fathers and Sons

Friel returns to nineteenth-century Russia after *The Communication Cord* for a treatment of Ivan Turgenev's novel, *Fathers and Sons* (first produced at the National Theatre, London, on 8 July 1987). Like *Three Sisters,* this novel is one of the classics of the nineteenth-century realist tradition, which identifies the writer as a social and cultural diagnostician, though not to the extent of expecting him to compromise his moral and aesthetic individuality. The appeal of such an identity to a writer in Friel's position is understandable, though it would belittle and distort his achievement to label him the Irish Turgenev; *Fathers and Sons* is very much a Friel play.

The play's title page states that it is "after the novel by Ivan Turgenev;"[51] it is not a translation in the obvious sense that *Three Sisters* was. Still, issues of language and communication remain very much to the fore, though they are subtly embedded in the action. Once again, the enactment of a world of discourse is assumed as the basis of drama. The dramatic conflict in *Fathers and Sons* consists of the discrepancy between the apparent finality of language and the flux of nonverbal areas of being.

The play faithfully follows the novel's story line, though a certain amount of compression is inevitable. The story tells of two students returning home from university: Arkady Nikolayevich Kirsanov, who has just graduated, and Yevgeny Vassilyich Bazarov, who still has to complete his medical studies. First they visit Arkady's family, then Bazarov's. They have hardly arrived, however, before they identify themselves as nihilists—espousers, that is, of the latest philosophical line whose objective is to "remake Russia" (12). Bazarov, at least as far as his language goes, is the personification of the stern rigor necessary for such a task; Arkady is his voluble, amiable acolyte. The play goes on to show the fate of such a philosophy once it is tested outside the laboratory conditions of university life.

That life is not a theory has already been suggested by the irregular arrangements in Arkady's home. His father, Nikolai, whose signature phrase is "Now let us organize our lives," has manifestly succumbed to some spirit other than that of organization; he has fathered a child with one of his retainers, Fenichka. And as though to reinforce the influential place of emotional waywardness in the scheme of things, the other important member of the Kirsanov household, foppish Francophile Uncle Pavel, is said to have been the victim of à passionate affair in his youth. (Bazarov is particularly hostile to what appears to be Pavel's affectations, lacking the imaginative sympathy to see how harmless he is.) Thus it is not surprising that when two ladies from a neighboring estate present themselves Bazarov and Arkady are affected by their presence. Arkady falls for Katya Sergeyevna. But Bazarov "has misunderstood the whole situation" (54) between himself and Anna Sergeyevna Odintsov.

For the first time he has encountered contradictory feelings that he cannot rationalize away. Now his sense that "he is an outsider politically and socially" (8) does not serve him well, nor do the heroic terms in which Arkady describes him: "Only Bazarov is a fully authentic revolutionary. Only Bazarov has the courage and the clarity of purpose to live outside ordinary society, without attachments, beyond the consolation of emotions" (45). So clearly convinced has he become of his own verbal construct, his nihilism, that he has forgotten the force of Nikolai's observation that "we all have our codes. We all have our masks" (16). That *we all*—which, as Nikolai's remark implies, embraces a collectivity of differences—is a phenomenon to which Bazarov, for philosophical reasons, does not give adequate credit. Fenichka and the servant Dunyasha may make fun of Pavel, calling him "the Tailor's Dummy" because of his impeccable dress, but at the same time they accept him: their mockery is not tantamount to cultural erasure. Bazarov, on the other hand, is one-dimensional in his aggressively rude exposition of Pavel's effete image. Pavel is presumably an example of someone who would suffer from the "force" that Bazarov shruggingly says will be used "if necessary" (12) in order to remake the world in the image of nihilism.

It is an irony characteristic of the original and underlined by Friel's treatment that Pavel is the source of Bazarov's ultimate humiliation, and that the pretext for the humiliation is Bazarov allowing his emotions to get the better of him with Fenichka. Accidentally seeing the small, touching moment between Fenichka and Bazarov, Pavel challenges rhe student to a duel, evincing a code from the bygone age to which Pavel temperamentally belongs. Dueling may be a dubious form of judgment to a rationalist like Bazarov (who is unable to shoot), but it is one of those usages, sanctified by tradition, that defy reason and govern life, just as emotional attachments do.

In the event, Pavel is accidentally wounded, but it is Bazarov who is defeated. He returns to his father's house and dies tending the typhus-ridden peasants he despises. This eminently avoidable death compounds the role of the irrational in the story. Bazarov helps those he hates. They need his help because of typhus, a disaster that, like most others that flesh is heir to, may not be merely verbalized away or contained by apparently watertight rational constructs. As the play's conclusion implies, the alternatives to Bazarov's revolution are the mutuality and continuity represented by Arkady's wedding to Katya and his inheritance of the Kirsanov estate. With regard to the unpredictability and contradictoriness of life, it is best to acknowledge it, celebrate it; thus Nikolai, at last, marries Fenichka. The word-giving of marriage is at once more enlightened, more natural, and more adequate an image of human potential than Bazarov's approval of the circumstances at the beginning of the play, when he demands, "Who needs marriage?" (17).

Fathers and Sons offers a reprise of many of Friel's most persistent preoccupations. The conflict between youth and age has been in his work since *To This Hard House;* the problem of translating word into action has been present since *A Sort of Freedom;* the urge to judge and the need for tolerance has received numerous vivid embodiments, beginning with *The Gentle Island.* In addition, with Bazarov, Friel presents his definitive outsider figure. Yet it is noteworthy that the outsider himself is now critically situated with regard to his world; a nihilist, defined by Arkady, is "someone who looks at everything critically" (10). Bazarov retains some of the exemplary features of his comrades in Friel's oeuvre, such as their intensity and their sense of principle. But he lacks their irony and their capacity to improvise. He is in love with his own language. Earlier Friel outsiders tend to exploit their satirical possession of the language of others.

In addition, *Fathers and Sons* can be thought of as a distillation of *Three Sisters* and *The Communication Cord.* The note of continuance that *Three Sisters* sounds, and that is heard in Olga's opening recollection of their father's funeral ("The clock struck twelve then too")⁵² , is here heard in the wedding bells that close the play. The squandering of emotional energy that is typical of the farcical proceedings in *The Communication Cord* is here given a more somber representation. It may be difficult to like Bazarov, but it is even more difficult not to be moved by his fate—a complex of reactions that summarize Friel's interest in *Fathers and Sons.* Yet Bazarov's fate is the outcome of the sense of language that Jack McNeilis and Senator Doctor Donovan share, a sense that language is the author of life, rather than an imperfect instrument that—in terms established by *The Communication Cord*—is at its most expressive, most inscrutable, and least articulate when least verbal, which is at moments of "response cries."

Friel's language plays provide very strong evidence of the playwright's desire to have his characters override their textual confines. Defining themselves by language, or permitting this to occur, tends to varieties of ossification. Behind every verbal construct lies a silence out of which an alternative meaning to the text emerges, a meaning that is more than words can say, a meaning that is preverbal and that returns the characters to a more fundamental level of their being than the syntactical presumption of order can reach. The dance of language finally yields to a moment of stasis, a moment of completeness, a moment of superior articulation. The destruction of Frank Hardy lies on the far side of his words and articulates the self-destructive expressiveness of his career. The silence that descends on the Irish language is heard in *Translations* behind the gallant, doomed verbiage of Hugh. In *Three Sisters,* the silence of empty lives is heard beyond the brave but desolating sound of both the departing military band and Solyony's fatal pistol shot. The kiss in *The Communication Cord* is the sound of silence. More subtly in *Fathers and Sons,* the silence is what we never learn of Anna's vigil by Bazarov's deathbed and her precipitate, undecorous departure, the counterpart in politesse of the young man's death. That silence is articulated in the halting, inappropriate narrative in which Bazarov's father tells Arkady the news of his friend's death. And, as *Fathers and Sons* suggests in its ending, this silence demands to be drowned by brave rituals honoring the promise of life.

Making History

In *Making History*, which received its premiere at the Guildhall, Derry, on 20 September 1988, Friel again dramatizes a decisive turning point in Irish history, as he did in *Translations*. Set in Elizabethan Ireland, the play deals with the attempts of the old Gaelic polity to resist being overwhelmed by the forces of England and Englishness. The principal architect of that resistance was Hugh O'Neill, Earl of Tyrone and the play's protagonist.

The action focuses on the buildup to, and the aftermath of, the battle that decided the fate of the native Irish as a politically autonomous and culturally distinct entity. This battle, fought in 1601 at the port of Kinsale, in southern Ireland, was between the forces of Elizabeth and those of O'Neill, the latter reinforced by a Spanish expedition. Though the Spanish presence did not materially affect the short-lived course of the Battle of Kinsale, its existence draws attention to the larger context in which O'Neill's resistance took place. The context is that of Counter-Reformation Europe, of whose militant spirit O'Neill is perceived to be a champion—by the anti-English, anti-Protestant Spanish throne; by the Pope; and, not least, as the play makes clear, by Archbishop Peter Lombard, Primate of All Ireland, and the author of a hagiographic biography of O'Neill. It is this authorial activity that makes the play's title typically double-edged. O'Neill is the powerful historical actor. But for his actions to be appreciated, they require installation in a text. The requirements of a text, both in terms of its conventions and of its likely readership, are such that a rhetoric of attainment is articulated rather than a truthful narrative. As the play brings out, there is an irreconcilable difference between history actually made on the battlefield and history made by the historian.

Making History is in two acts, each with two scenes. The play opens in 1591, ten years before the Battle of Kinsale, and it ends in Rome, with O'Neill, his faithful retainer and private secretary, Harry Hoveden, and Peter Lombard, in exile—an exile begun in 1607 and known in Irish history as the Flight of the Earls. The other two main characters in the play are O'Neill's third wife, Mabel Bagenal, and the other well-known earl who also took flight, Hugh O'Donnell, Earl of Tyrconnell. The titles of the two Irish nobles have a number of important connotations. In the first place, as earls, they bear English titles. These were conferred on them by the English crown, in exchange for vows of loyalty and obedience to the imperial regime, which sought either to make puppets of them or to supplant them. The facts of the historical case bear out ambiguities of nomenclature, and the uncertainties they underwrite, that inform the play's intellectual framework. Moreover, bearing in mind that Tyrconnell is the old Irish name for the territory roughly corresponding to present-day County Donegal, the play returns Friel to his original landscape and to considerations of loyalty and dividedness, action and alienation, which he first broached in the Donegal and Tyrone of his short stories. In addition, the play offers a reminder of the crucial presence of Ulster in Irish history.

The play opens with a recognizable Friel scenario. O'Neill is tending to matters of simple pleasure—arranging flowers—while Hoveden recites reports of squabbles and problems among the families within the chief's, or earl's, jurisdiction. (The text sustains throughout a complex metaphor drawing on nature, breeding, cultivation, culture, and related—interrelated— phenomena. This metaphor is a means of introducing issues of race, landholding, development, and hybridization, which are clearly germane to the action's imperialistic context and to the play's intellectual dimension, but which do not disturb the work's dramatic structure.) The contrast between the private and momentary represented by O'Neill and the public and ongoing contained in Hoveden's reports is arrestingly brought to a head with the entrance of Lombard and O'Donnell: as Lombard is detailing the results of his European lobbying on behalf of the Irish Catholic cause, O'Neill announces that he has just remarried.

Clearly the marital career of a chieftain is no small consideration, as every reader of Shakespeare will readily recall. The fact that the forty-one-year-old O'Neill's new wife is barely twenty is, therefore, a much less scandalous circumstance than the fact that she is an "upstart." She is Mabel Bagenal, daughter of one of the new breed of Elizabethan settlers, and sister of Sir Henry Bagenal, the Queen's Marshal in Ulster. She is a Protestant, and O'Neill is nominally a Catholic. The marriage, therefore, crosses cultural, political, and religiously sectarian lines. Yet, as the play goes on to establish, the possibilities that the marriage establishes at the private level have no future in the world of public events (Mabel's death in childbirth, following the catastrophe of Kinsale, confirms the play's sense of historical impasse and is reminiscent of the birth and death of the infant offstage in *Translations*).

Mabel is another of Friel's impressive female characters, vulnerable though resilient, intellectually and emotionally acute, candid and passionate.

The play's second scene shows her to best advantage, beginning with a dialogue with her sister Mary, who has come to Mabel's new home with a mistaken view to coaxing her back. As the scene develops, however, it becomes clear that not even Mabel has fully comprehended what marriage to O'Neill entails. Friel skillfully uses the presence of Mary, who is loyal to the "upstart" dispensation, as a means whereby her unlikely brother-in-law can reveal his own irrevocable decision to rebel against the crown, for all that he is, by virtue of his title, one of that crown's upholders. It is in her arguments against her husband's rebellion that Mabel has her finest hour, all to no avail: virtually the next mention of her name is in connection with her death in childbed.

Since the play concerns itself with prelude and aftermath, it is pertinent to add the historical note that the rebellion upon which O'Neill embarks at the end of the first act lasted from 1595 to 1603 and, judged from a purely military standpoint, rates as the most sustained and successful of all Irish encounters with the British army, a fact the Kinsale debacle tends to overshadow. It is Kinsale, however, that seals the fate of O'Neill and of the Celtic, native Ireland to which he remained faithful, despite the blandishments of earlhood and a youth of fosterage among the English nobility. In the name of that loyalty, he indites an abject surrender to the crown, hoping that he will be allowed to remain with his defeated people. But it is not to be; instead he recites his testament of submission in haunting counterpoint to Peter Lombard's grandiose representation of him as the conventional historical hero, a *pius Aeneas,* the depth and character of whose *pietas* Lombard finds to be beside the historiographic point. The unification of those two dissonant codes that closes the play, coming as it does after a thorough depiction of O'Neill's degraded and paralyzing life of Roman exile, functions as a brilliant crystallization of the play's preoccupations. Each of the speakers is deaf to the other and speaks without deliberateness and unavailingly to that deafness. History is the sound of both voices intermingled, and of many others besides, foremost among them, as far as this play is concerned, that of Mabel Bagenal. Making history—the process of distillation to which culture, ideology, and political opportunism together in uneasy synthesis subject events—requires that one tonality be louder than another, that one characterization of events prevail. The process preserves and distorts (by immobilizing) the maker of history in the active sense of the term, as though life cannot be considered complete without the application of the embalmer's cosmetics.

Making History shows Friel both moving back to some of the concerns with history, culture, and language that formed the basis of his finest work in the 1970s, and moving forward, by enlarging the scope of those concerns. Not since *The Enemy Within,* where the author explicitly eschewed history, has Friel directed his attention to an important figure in Irish history, and in none of his plays has he addressed the subjects of historical action self-consciously undertaken and historiography deliberately commissioned. Thus, once again, a Friel play manages both to relate to its predecessors and to depart from them. In addition, and more importantly, *Making History* modifies the image of the human found in most of its forerunners. The sense in which O'Neill is the victim of circumstances that he brought about is very much to the fore, largely because of the enormous consequences that result from those circumstances. In this respect, he is a typical Friel protagonist. The difference here is the degree of deliberateness with which he finally commits himself to action, an awareness as complete and committed in its own way as that of Lombard the historiographer. It is O'Neill's commitment, enhanced by his own consciousness of what it entails, that confers on him the dignity and integrity imparted by Friel to all his protagonists. When seen in the context of such enhanced commitment, the earl's defeat is perhaps merely the familiar consequent of making history.

Chapter Five

The Theater of Brian Friel

Friel's sequence of language plays, which may tentatively be said to culminate in *Fathers and Sons*,[1] apart from its obvious significance in itself and the interest of each of the play's subjects, illustrates what might be described as the sequence principle in Friel's overall output. Beginning with characterizations of the emotional and social life of Ballybeg (the character sequence), Friel's career develops with plays set outside Ballybeg (the collectivist, or ensemble, sequence), before modulating into the language sequence.

Such a generalized sketch raises more questions than it answers, including ones about the possibility of seeing Friel's plays not as sequences but as pairs—the Russian pair, the *Translations* and *The Communication Cord* pair, the pair in *Lovers,* the *Philadelphia* and *The Enemy Within* pair, the family pair of *Living Quarters* and *Aristocrats,* the public pair of *Freedom* and *Volunteers.*[2] Whether they are considered in sequences or in pairs, the general picture emerges of plays which are both related to, and distinct from, each other. Each possesses its own unique way of treating themes they all share, and to which each of them gives new, refined, definitions. The options presented by Bazarov and Arkady, the potential for making sense that those two characters contrastingly and jointly embody, are present in Private Gar and Public Gar. And the coexistence, interdependence, and conversational brio of these two characters in *Philadelphia, Here I Come!* may be seen in the relationship between Arkady and Bazarov. These conditions not only obtain in the human, personal relations between the twin protagonists of *Fathers and Sons,* they extend into other relationships in the play—between Nikolai and Pavel, for example, and between Arkady and Bazarov's father, Vassily Ivanyich.

Considering *Philadelphia* and *Fathers and Sons* together is useful for a number of reasons. It is a reminder of the variety of settings in Friel's plays. It draws attention to his work's emotional, intellectual, and cultural growth. Being an adaptation, *Fathers and Sons* underlines Friel's formal skills, as does his choreography of the large cast. And, as noted, the two plays exemplify Friel's remarkable thematic consistency. It does not seem too much to say that Friel's oeuvre is a tribute to the author's tenacity and integrity, as well as to his range and growth. He has remained faithful to his preoccupations, just as he has been loyal to his native territory. (There may well be an important connection between the two forms of attachment, a possibility that *Translations,* in particular, raises).

Friel's range can be characterized in a number of ways. One, already noted, is simply the plays' widely differing settings. In view of the prominence of Ballybeg, range of locales may seem a contradictory claim to make for Friel's work. Nevertheless, it is still a long way from the island of Iona to the general store of S. B. O'Donnell and out again to the island of Ireland in *The Mundy Scheme.* On the face of it, nineteenth-century Donegal seems very different from nineteenth-century Russia. But, and perhaps this is one of the ideals around which all Friel's work is structured, contrast does not necessarily mean conflict; on the contrary it may be the basis for a more conscious, deliberate mutuality. (The prominence of love and community in his plays suggest the scope, depth, and simplicity of that ideal: his characters, wherever we find them, are implicated in the difficulty of living with themselves as well as with others, of living with themselves *through* living with others).

Friel's use of Ballybeg illustrates in its own way interconnections, contrast, and compatibility. It is never the same Ballybeg; it is always the same Ballybeg. The Ballybeg in *Living Quarters* is the complement of the one in *Aristocrats,* and the same is true of the two places in *Translations* and *The Communication Cord.* The associations and connotations of the place itself—its remoteness, its pedestrian ethos, its inspiration to exile—constitute a flexible space (a stage) where the human implications of its reality can be explored.

Another example of Friel's range is that while most of his plays call for male protagonists, the author never forgets that there are two genders. *Faith Healer* is a particularly graphic case in point. Grace lacks the bravado and earthiness of some of Friel's women characters, but she persuasively embodies the emotional tenacity of an Anna Butler, Sarah Sweeney, or Cass McGuire, and like them she is a victim of male illusion, male talk. Like such illustrious predecessors in Irish theater as J. M. Synge and Sean O'Casey, Friel shows the imaginative sympathy necessary to create female characters who are dramatically vital. Yet Cass McGuire, for example, is not only a wonderful stage creation, but also an embodiment of emotional freedom, of a desire to speak in her own language, of resistance to the twin rationales of repression and illusion. Her defeat should not diminish her importance, any more than that of other marginalized outsiders, such as Keeney and the men in *Volunteers,* should diminish theirs. Friel is not offering a token "wonderful part for a woman." His female characters speak for themselves as credible, individuated exponents of his vision.

Friel's female protagonists, however, are much rarer than his youthful male ones, the frequent presence of which are another source of unity and diversity in his output. From Gar O'Donnell to Bazarov, youth plays a big part in Friel's perspective on his material. One reason for this choice is that the characters' vitality does not appear exceptional, nor does it have to justify itself. Another is that such characters are in a state of flux, given their age and their strangely paradoxical social status, which denotes them as presently marginal but potentially all-important. This minority status is enhanced by Friel through his casting many of his youthful protagonists in the role of outsider. Here again, Friel is not being tokenistic. His interest is not, even when dealing with a character like Skinner in *The Freedom of the City*, in the problems of contemporary youth or some such editorial page commonplace. His youths typically offer a focus on private dramas, the dramas of all our lives, rather than the sociological and cultural problems of temporary members of a social caste.

The continuing presence of Friel's youths is consistent with the continuing presence of the family in his work, even in works as different from each other as *Living Quarters* and *Translations*. The family setting enables Friel continually to review perennial (and not particularly, certainly not exclusively, Irish) problems connected with the necessary human project of tolerating others. Love, the need for others, coexistence, dependence, independence, mutual tolerance, and respect: these are the areas Friel can consider by focusing on a youthful protagonist in a family setting. Very often the family's human ecology is shown under threat from external, impersonal contaminants, as in the familial bonding in *The Freedom of the City* and *Volunteers*. It is his persistent attempts to reveal images of the human, images that articulate an innate emotional power through their unsuccessful resistance to cultural and institutional impositions, that give Friel's work its depth and consistency.

Friel's growth is obviously related to his range. Clearly the later plays, the plays of the 1970s and 1980s, are more verbally sophisticated and intellectually critical than their forerunners. Extension of range entails development of artistic resources and technical skills. As has been noted earlier, Friel's technical experiments take place at the same time as his early successes. Thus the plays written in the 1970s and 1980s may seem technically sedate after a work as elaborate as *The Loves of Cass McGuire*. But the technical adventurousness of *Philadelphia, Here I Come!* and its immediate successors is still present in, for example, *The Freedom of the City* and *Living Quarters*. The difference is that technique is more closely wed to overall effect in the later plays, as a comparison between the role of the Commentators in *Lovers* and that of Sir in *Living Quarters* readily illustrates. And *Faith Healer* owes nothing to earlier Friel plays in term of technical daring.

In particular, Friel's use of the two-act play (*Freedom, Volunteers, Living Quarters*) introduces the facade of an open-and-shut case, promising exposition and resolution, only to produce quite different effects of repetition and intensification. The two-act structure is extremely well-suited to Friel's essentially static, verbal theater where whatever a situation contains has already been determined, and where what takes place on stage is a stylized enactment and crystallization of those contents. Yet it is also important to bear in mind that Friel does not consistently conform to any particular formal pattern: *Translations* is a standard three-acter.

Ritual, depending as it does on repetition and restraint, is an important dimension of Friel's theater in bringing into being the epiphanous effect of crystallization. Friel's characters are frequently engaged in ritualistic or ritualized activities, and are perhaps increasingly so: *Three Sisters* reveals how much of life is susceptible to ritual (though this susceptibility may be more Chekhov than Friel), while it could be argued that *Fathers and Sons* is a play about rituals transgressed by Bazarov. Ritual also conveys continuance, both culturally and individualistically speaking. Indeed, rituals permit the individual to submit freely to a cultural event that serves not only individual but also collective needs. One of the most potent secular institutions that promote the mutually illuminating intersection of the individual and the collective is the theater.

What ritual accomplishes artistically for Friel, fate seems to accomplish intellectually. In *Translations,* Owen interrupts Yolland's account of himself, his background, and his fortuitous presence in Ireland, by asking: "Do you believe in fate?"[3] It seems a strange question at the time, and an unlikely one for the ostensibly superficial Owen. Its force is to suggest a sense of self-awareness and resignation on Owen's part about what he, like his father, perceives to be the inevitable progress of history. Yolland does not answer the question; it is as if he has not heard it. There seems to be a connection between his lack of awareness and the reckless way in which he gives himself to his Irish experiences. Yolland's naiveté argues for the nonexistence of an impersonal force directing his affairs. Such naiveté also leads him to disregard his essential strangeness, encoded in his language and in his military uniform, with fatal consequences. Yet if Owen believes in such a manipulating force, he ends his part in the play by apparently going out to resist it. As in *Living Quarters,* even if a character allows for the presence of fate, the idea does not negate the desire for freedom. This thought also informs the image of Lily,

Michael, and Skinner at the conclusion of *The Freedom of the City,* and animates *The Loves of Cass McGuire.*

Ritual is a tacit commission of and identification with pattern and custom. Fate—the way things are, rather than the way a character might make them—is the exploitation of ritualists' passivity by powers they cannot placate. Again, *Translations* offers an illustration of the point. The baby whose christening Hugh attends in act 1 dies in act 3. Both events are ritualistically observed. The second one, however, like other silencings the play suggests, is not the result of a specific human agent. It is part of a hostile, alien, disordering force. Its reality resides in its incomprehensibility. It is a foreign language. Ritual is the means whereby form pacifies fate, making it both recognizable and containable.

It is on the subject of dramatic form that Friel has received some of his most serious criticism. Friel has obviously given a great deal of time and thought to what he has called "this happy fusion that occurs so seldom between content and form . . . there's no point in discussing them separately."[4] Form is also the subject of an appraisal of Friel made by Denis Johnston, the one Irish playwright to come of age, technically and intellectually speaking, in the 1930s. There is, therefore, inevitable connotations of mantle-passing in what is said, however unfortunate or unintended they may have been.

After splitting the mantle between Friel and Hugh Leonard (another Irish playwright to make his name in the 1960s, though his work does not have the penetration of Friel's or of two other notable, but less well-known, Irish playwrights of the same generation, Thomas Kilroy and Thomas Murphy), Johnston goes on to state his case as follows:

This is the day of the Situation Pieces that are usually as free of a story line as Goldilocks and her Three Bears. We must now expect merely to wait for Godot with tickets to Philadelphia in our hands. . . . Third Acts are not now concerned with living happily or miserably ever after, but more usually with the job of getting back to the opening lines of the First Act. The form is circular, and does not noticeably recognise the old formula of a Beginning, Middle and an End. Indeed, we are somewhat nervous about Endings and do not wish to brood too much upon what is just around the corner. . . . In all of this Friel is in the forefront of the Irish Theatre, and clearly deserves his success.[5]

This appraisal of Friel is in effect a backhanded tribute to the change in Irish drama that Friel's work represents. Friel's plays belong to the theater of the turning point, or rather, the theater of the point of no return. As such, it is clearly at odds with the theater of denoument, which is what Johnston prefers, and of which he is an accomplished and culturally significant exponent. Because of what it understands to be drama, however, Friel's work can dispense with plot. Thus, for example, it takes an objective, distanced, wistfully ironic view of the role of accident, contradiction, and sudden revelation in the lives of its characters. It speaks on behalf of its characters' inner lives rather for their social existence. It is a critic of the kitchen's violence, rather than an endorser of the drawing room's politesse. It dwells on conditions, rather than develops stories.

For this reason, it tends to concentrate on decisive moments—moments of change, moments of revelation, moments of definitiveness. The drama of such a theater inheres in the difference between the flux of characters' behaviour and the fact that for all that flux's energy and waywardness it will culminate in one irreversible circumstance. This is not the theater of change but the theater of change's prelude and aftermath. It concentrates, therefore, on buildup and letdown, on both the distillation and enlargement of the crucial moment.

Friel's own words describe his achievement: "I would like to write a play that would capture the peculiar spiritual, and indeed material, flux that this country is in at the moment. This has got to be done, for me anyway, and I think it has got to be done at a local, parochial level, and hopefully this will have meaning for other people in other countries."[6] Since this statement was made in 1970, Friel has realized his ambition in play after play. And the interesting word *capture* speaks directly to the flexibility of form that has succeeded in embodying his concerns. His capturing of flux speaks to the need to contain it, to make it culturally relevant and spiritually productive. It speaks to the artist's dream of attaining freedom by imposing form.

Friel's mention of "this country" is a reminder of his cultural significance. Unlike many writers in other countries, the Irish writer is partly significant for his artistic attainments and partly for the way in which he addresses questions of cultural value and cultural tradition. There has yet to be an Irish writer who did not have something to say about the character and quality of either Irish literature, Irish audiences, or Irish society; usually the comments take in all three subjects in one fell swoop. Friel is no exception, though his public statements on such matters have been fewer than most. Nevertheless, the following comment by Seamus Heaney in his review of *Translations* speaks to the cultural context of Friel's achievement. Heaney has been discussing Manus's gift of speech to Sarah, and Sarah's subsequent silencing by Lancey. He goes on: "It is as if some symbolic figure of Ireland from an eighteenth-century vision poem, the one who once confidently called herself Cathleen Ni Houlihan, has been struck dumb by the shock of modernity.

Friel's work, not just here but in his fourteen preceding plays, constitutes a powerful therapy, a set of imaginative exercises that give her the chance to know and say herself properly to herself again."[7]

It is possible that Friel would demur at being elevated to such an eminent spokesman's role. He has been at pains to keep his artistic life distinct from his life as a citizen, and in 1970 tried to distance himself as a dramatist from events in Northern Ireland: "I don't think I can write about . . . the situation in the North. Because, first of all, I am emotionally too much involved about it; secondly, because the thing is in transition at the moment. A play about the civil rights situation in the North won't be written, I hope, for another ten or fifteen years."[8] Events were to prove otherwise. And the upshot of writing *The Freedom of the City* and *Volunteers* was, as Seamus Deane has noted, to evoke critics' "ferocity and blindness . . . especially in London and New York. . . . Wisely, he ignored this hack reviewing, although it cost him dear financially, especially in New York. Instead, Friel kept his attention fixed on the evolving form of his own work."[9]

The quality of that attention, along with the scrupulous distinction Friel has attempted to maintain "between the Irishman who suffers and the artist's mind which creates,"[10] is the basis of Friel's cultural significance. Friel's plays, precisely because they do not, for the most part, deal with the immediacies of Irish life, either in the North or in the Republic, and because they do not actively take sides in the current introspective debate about the nature of, and prospect for, Irishness, act as illuminating analogues of the desires, confusions, and intransigences that the debates, and the violence in the North that to a large extent has prompted them, articulate.

The emphases in his work on division, mutuality, community, cliché, flux, claustrophobia, victimization, and inevitability are not present because of conditions in his native province, nor are they foreign to all other playwrights in other countries and at this and other periods. Friel was neither entirely formed by the North, nor are his works solely responses to conditions in the North. On the contrary, the fact that Friel is able to find a framework of discourse in which such concerns can be approached and apprehended makes his work an exception to the typical public use of language in Northern Ireland.

Friel may be regarded as a writer whose work desires to dispel the illusions of rhetoric and the finality of divisions. This desire is transmitted in its critique of culturally coded language, in its acknowledgment of human frailty with its need for consolation and annealment, in its delighted projection of spontaneity and naturalness. At a more fundamental level, the desire is expressed formally in the conception of plays premised on the apparent untenability of its central situation, a situation from which the protagonist needs to be delivered. Such a desire also informs a view Friel attributes to the audiences of the Abbey Theatre in its formative years, who "recognized then that the theatre was an important social element that not only reflected but shaped the society it served; that dramatists were revolutionary in the broadest sense of that word; and that subjective truth—the artist's truth—was dangerously independent of Church and State."[11]

The dramatist's revolution, if it occurs at all, takes place in the realm of perception. It reveals unsuspected realignments in the light of familiar inevitabilities, not as prescriptions ("dramatists have no solutions"[12]) but as potentialities. For an audience, seeing a play ratifies Friel's description of writing one: "The task of writing the play, the actual job of putting the pattern together, itself generates belief in the pattern. The act and the artifact sustain one another."[13] The articulation of pattern is a recognition of boundaries from a position outside boundaries. It is the combination of freedom and constraint that the playwright shares with the audience. It is the collective audience and each individual member of it: it is man and his world. This combination of opposites, this tension within wholeness, gives Friel's plays their momentum and significance. It renders his work symbolic of his place and people, while at the same time offering a far from localized conception of the human lot. Words describing the achievement of another Irish playwright, Oscar Wilde, apply with even greater appropriateness to the work of Brian Friel, and it is in the light of them that his plays might be, with most justice, appraised: "The object of life is not to simplify it. As our conflicting impulses coincide, as our repressed feelings vie with those we express, as our solid views disclose unexpected fissures, we are all secret dramatists, whether or not we bring our complexities onto the stage. In this light Wilde's [or Friel's] works become exercises in self-criticism as well as pleas for tolerance."[14]

Notes and References

Preface

1. Christopher Fitz-Simons, *The Irish Theatre* (London: Thames and Hudson, 1983), 193.
2. Robert Hogan, *After the Irish Renaissance* (Minneapolis: University of Minnesota Press, 1967), viii.
3. D. E. S. Maxwell, *Brian Friel* (Lewisburg, PA: Bucknell University Press, 1973), 109.
4. Ibid.
5. Des Hickey and Gus Smith, *A Paler Shade of Green* (London: Leslie Frewin, 1972), 221.
6. Elgy Gillespie, "The Saturday Interview: Brian Friel," *Irish Times*, 5 September 1981.
7. Hickey and Smith, *Paler Shade*, 222.
8. Seamus Deane, Introduction to *Brian Friel: Selected Plays* (Washington, D.C.: Catholic University of America Press, 1986), 22.
9. See Christopher Murray, "Irish Drama in Transition 1966–1978," *Etudes Irlandaises*, nouvelle serie 4, (December 1979): 287–308.

Chapter One

1. Graham Morison, "An Ulster Writer: Brian Friel," *Acorn*, Spring 1965: 14.
2. *Living Quarters* (London: Faber and Faber, 1978), 8.
3. Morison, "Friel," 10.
4. J. L. McCracken, "Northern Ireland (1921–66)," in *The Course of Irish History*, ed. T. W. Moody and F. X. Martin (Cork: Mercier Press, 1967), 320.
5. Hickey and Smith, *Paler Shade*, 221. For further information on Friel's early professional years in Derry and the effect of the city's atmosphere on him, see Maxwell, *Friel*, 18–31, and Ulf Dantanus, *Brian Friel: The Growth of an Irish Playwright* (Atlantic Highlands, N.J.: Humanities Press, 1985), 23–25.
6. Morison, "Friel," 4.
7. Tyrone Guthrie, *A Life in Theatre* (New York: Limelight Editions, 1985), 349.
8. Guthrie, *A Life*, 344.
9. Hickey and Smith, *Paler Shade*, 222.
10. Ibid.
11. Ibid.
12. Derek Mahon's treatments of Moliere's *School for Husbands* (entitled

High Time) and *The School for Wives,* Thomas Paulin's version of *Antigone, The Riot Act,* and Thomas Kilroy's *Double Cross* come immediately to mind.

13. *The Times* [London], 8 September.

14. "A Challenge to *Acorn,*" *Acorn* 14 (1970): 4.

15. Field Day Theatre Company, *Ireland's Field Day* (London: Hutchinson, 1985), vii. The preface has the collective signature of the Company, and the book reprints the first six Field Day pamphlets. There is an afterword by the critic Denis Donoghue. For more on Field Day, see John Gray, "Field Day Five Years On," *Linen Hall Review* 2, no. 2 (Summer 1985): 4–10.

16. A critique of Field Day may be found in Edna Longley, "Poetry and Politics in Northern Ireland," in *Poetry in the Wars* (Newcastle-upon-Tyne: Bloodaxe Books, 1986), 185–210.

17. "The Child," *The Bell* 18, no. 4 (July 1952): 232–33.

18. The stories are collected in *The Saucer of Larks* (Garden City, N.Y.: Doubleday, 1962) and *The Gold in the Sea* (Garden City, N.Y.: Doubleday, 1966). The source of quotations from individual stories are hereafter identified in the text by reference to either *SOL,* or *GIS,* followed by page number.

19. Walter Allen, *The Short Story in English* (New York: Oxford University Press, 1981), 389.

20. Maxwell, *Friel,* 31.

21. For a thorough discussion of this story and its Derry context, see Maxwell, *Friel,* 15–17.

22. Dantanus, *Friel,* 25.

23. Sean MacMahon, "The Black North: The Prose Writers of the North of Ireland," *Threshold* 21 (Summer 1967): 172.

24. John Wilson Foster, *Forces and Themes in Ulster Fiction* (Dublin: Gill and Macmillan, 1973), x.

25. Seamus Deane, "Brian Friel," *Ireland Today,* 978 (1981): 7.

26. Robert Lloyd Praeger, *The Way That I Went* (Dublin: Allen Figgis, 1969), 101.

27. Ibid., 22.

28. Dantanus, *Friel,* 56.

29. Ibid., 52.

30. Tyrone Guthrie, *In Various Directions: A View of the Theatre* (London: Michael Joseph, 1963), 113.

31. Frank O'Connor, *The Lonely Voice* (New York: Harper & Row, 1985), 18. O'Connor considered the concept applicable to the short story generally speaking: it has, however, a peculiarly apt application to the Irish short story.

32. *Epiphany*—defined by James Joyce as "a sudden spiritual manifestation"—is perhaps the most important term in the modern short story's critical vocabulary. See James Joyce, *Stephen Hero* (London: Jonathan Cape, 1969), 216–17.

33. Walter Allen, *The Short Story,* 389.

34. Foster, *Ulster Fiction,* 255.

35. This phrase comes from Shakespeare's *Midsummer Night's Dream* (3.2.9.), where it describes Bottom the weaver and his companions.
36. Maxwell, *Friel*, 17.
37. For a similar example of the significance of this dependence see "The Flower of Killymore" (*GIS*, 129–44).
38. Foster, *Ulster Fiction*, 69.
39. Seamus Deane, Introduction to *Brian Friel: Selected Stories* (Dublin: Gallery Press, 1979), 13.
40. Another notable Friel story about the power and need—the apparently natural inevitability—of illusion is "The Gold in the Sea" (*GIS*, 91–102).
41. In this regard, it is interesting to consider the degree to which the poem "The Diviner" by Friel's friend, Seamus Heaney, may be considered a metaphor for *his* artistic practice. See Seamus Heaney, "The Diviner," in *Death of a Naturalist* (London: Faber and Faber, 1966), 36. On the poem's origins, see Heaney, *Preoccupations* (New York: Farrar, Straus and Giroux, 1980), 47–48.
42. Foster, *Ulster Fiction*, 72.
43. Maxwell, *Friel*, 31.
44. Pascal, *Pensées*, trans. W. F. Trotter (New York: E. P. Dutton, 1958), 61.
45. Seamus Heaney, "Song," in *Field Work* (London: Faber and Faber, 1979), 56.
46. Winston Churchill, *The World Crisis* (New York: Scribner's 1957), 5:336.
47. Seamus Deane, Introduction to *Stories*, 9.
48. For a fascinating, prescient discussion of the theatrical aspects of "Foundry House," see Maxwell, *Friel*, 40–41.
49. My thinking on this issue owes a great deal to Professor Anthony Bradley's unpublished essay, "Filiation and Affiliation in the Plays of Brian Friel."
50. *Philadelphia, Here I Come!* (New York: Farrar, Straus and Giroux), 25.
51. Dantanus, *Friel*, 14.
52. Cf. T. S. Eliot, *Notes Towards the Definition of Culture:* "The reader must remind himself as the author has constantly to do, of how much is here embraced by the term. It includes all the characteristic activities and interests of a people: Derby Day, Henley Regatta, Cowes, the twelfth of August, a cup final, the dog races, the pin table. . . . The reader can make his own list." Excerpted in *The Selected Prose of T. S. Eliot*, ed. Frank Kermode (New York: Harcourt Brace Jovanovich/Farrar, Straus and Giroux, 1975), 297–98.
53. A particularly good example of this type is Terry Bryson in the otherwise somewhat sketchy story, "Straight from his Colonial Success." (*SOL*, 156–67).

Chapter Two

1. Untitled essay in *Enter Certain Players: Edwards-MacLiammoir and the Gate 1928–1978*, ed. Peter Luke (Dublin: Dolmen Press, 1978), 23.
2. See Sam Hanna Bell, *The Theatre in Ulster* (Dublin: Gill and Macmillan, 1972), for a confirmation of this generalization and for exceptions to it.

3. Maxwell, *Friel*, 20.

4. These are the words of James B. Fagan, Tyrone Guthrie's first theatrical mentor. Quoted in James Forsyth, *Tyrone Guthrie: A Biography* (London: Hamish Hamilton, 1976), 45. Guthrie, of course, was Friel's most important theatrical mentor.

5. For the artistic and cultural importance of radio drama, see Peter Lewis, ed., *Radio Drama* (London: Longmans, 1981) and John Drakakis, ed., *British Radio Drama* (Cambridge: Cambridge University Press, 1981).

6. Although these four plays are examined here in detail and are Friel's most substantial contributions to the form, they do not comprise his total output for radio. For a discussion of Friel's minor pieces for radio, see Dantanus, *Friel*, 103–8.

7. *A Sort of Freedom*, typescript, 29; further citations noted parenthetically in text.

8. Maxwell, *Friel*, 49.

9. Ibid.

10. Ibid., 50.

11. *To This Hard House*, typescript, 4; further citations noted parenthetically in text.

12. Dantanus, *Friel*, 89.

13. Ibid., 92.

14. *A Doubtful Paradise*, typescript, 11; further citations noted parenthetically in text.

15. Maxwell, *Friel*, 51.

16. Dantanus, *Friel*, 93–94.

17. Maxwell, *Friel*, 52.

18. Dantanus, *Friel*, 94.

19. *The Blind Mice*, typescript, 48; further citations noted parenthetically in text.

20. Maxwell, *Friel*, 54.

21. Dantanus, *Friel*, 78.

22. *The Enemy Within* (Dublin: Gallery Press, 1979), 7.

23. Ibid., 72; further citations noted parenthetically in text.

24. Maxwell, *Friel*, 60.

25. Ibid., 56.

26. Dantanus, *Friel*, 115.

27. Morison, "Friel," 8.

28. Dantanus, *Friel*, 110.

29. Discussion of *The Enemy Within* can be found in Maxwell, *Friel*, 54–60, and in Dantanus, *Friel*, 110–15. The play was produced on BBC television in 1965. Generally speaking, *The Enemy Within* marks Friel's transition from broadcast media to live theater (Although he did write one more play for television [with David Hammond], *Farewell to Ardstrawn*, which was broadcast on BBC-TV in 1976.)

30. *Philadelphia, Here I Come!*, 17.

31. Maxwell, *Friel,* 63.
32. Hogan, *Irish Renaissance,* 197.

Chapter Three

1. A. W., "Introducing Brian Friel," *Acorn* 14 (1970): 27.
2. Morison, "Friel," 8.
3. Maxwell, *Friel,* 62.
4. Ibid., 70.
5. Robert Hogan, *"Since O'Casey" and Other Essays* (Gerrards Cross; Colin Smythe; Totowa, N.J.: Barnes and Noble, 1983), 129.
6. "The Theatre of Hope and Despair," *Everyman* 1 (1968): 21.
7. Maxwell, *Friel,* 55.
8. Ibid., 26.
9. Dantanus, *Friel,* 128.
10. *The Loves of Cass McGuire* (New York: Noonday Press, 1967), 11; further citations noted parenthetically in text.
11. Maxwell, *Friel,* 71.
12. Ibid., 76.
13. Ibid., 74.
14. Hogan, *O'Casey,* 129.
15. *Winners,* the first of the two plays, was perhaps inspired by one of Guthrie's little-known plays, *The Flowers Are Not for You to Pick.* "The dramatic framework . . . is the flashing before him of a young clergyman's life in the last moments before he drowns," according to Forsyth, *Guthrie,* 90.
16. *Lovers* (London: Faber and Faber, 1969), 5; further citations noted parenthetically in text.
17. That Joe and Mag are nonswimmers who die in a boating accident is an expression of their blithe foolhardiness, and of their inability to foresee their future, much as they may verbalize it. Thus it seems there is a basis for concluding that their deaths are accidental, not suicide; D. E. S. Maxwell claims, "whether [their deaths are] by accident or suicide is left open and is, according to Friel, irrelevant." Maxwell, *Friel,* 78.
18. Ibid., 80.
19. Dantanus, *Friel,* 138.
20. *Crystal and Fox and The Mundy Scheme* (New York: Farrar, Straus and Giroux, 1970), 27; further citations noted parenthetically in text.
21. Hogan, *O'Casey,* 130.
22. Dantanus, *Friel,* 140.
23. Maxwell, *Friel,* 88.
24. *Irish Literature,* ed. Justin McCarthy et al. (New York: Bigelow, Smith, n.d.), 3:1093.
25. *Crystal and Fox and The Mundy Scheme,* 157.

26. The reference here is to the activists who, in the rebellion of Easter 1916, fired the first shots in the struggle for Ireland's political independence from England.

27. Hickey and Smith, *Paler Shade*, 223.

28. Maxwell, *Friel*, 87.

29. *The Gentle Island* (London: Davis-Poynter, 1973), 9; further citations noted parenthetically in text.

30. Maxwell, *Friel*, 99–100.

31. This folksy apothegm also may be applied to the play's sense of language, or rather to the sense of language implicit in Shane's various mimetic set pieces. Thus, for example, the name Inishkeen may indeed mean "gentle island" (in Irish, *inis caoin*), or as Shane glibly says, "it's an Apache name. Means scalping island" (19)—in Irish, *inis scian* (knife island). A knife is what Sarah first proposes to use to avenge herself on Shane, and Manus (in itself a pun: the familiar name of a local saint and the Latin noun for hand) lost his arm to knife-wielders.

Chapter Four

1. "The Theatre of Hope and Despair," *Everyman* 1 (1968): 22.

2. Maxwell, *Friel*, 100.

3. Dantanus, *Friel*, 148.

4. Forsyth, *Guthrie*, 90.

5. Maxwell, *Friel*, 99.

6. For a treatment of the relationship between *The Freedom of the City* and its background, see Elizabeth Hale Winkler, "Brian Friel's *The Freedom of the City*: Historical Actuality and Dramatic Imagination," *Canadian Journal of Irish Studies* 7, no. 1 (June 1981): 12–31.

7. The analytical and journalistic literature of civil strife in Northern Ireland is voluminous. The following works may be mentioned as germane to conditions in Derry and helpful for an overview of the historical roots of the conflict: Eamon McCann, *War and an Irish Town* (Harmondsworth: Penguin Books, 1974), and Frank Curran, *Derry: Countdown to Disaster* (Dublin: Gill and Macmillan, 1986), both dealing with Derry in particular; Michael Farrell, *Northern Ireland: The Orange State* (London: Pluto Press, 1976), Dervla Murphy, *A Place Apart* (Harmondsworth: Penguin Books, 1979), and Liam de Paor, *Divided Ulster* (Harmondsworth: Penguin Books, 1970). Another work of literature besides *The Freedom of the City* written in response to the events of Bloody Sunday is Thomas Kinsella's poem, *Butchers Dozen: A Lesson for the Octave of Widgery* (Dublin: Peppercannister Press, 1972), reprinted in Kinsella, *Peppercannister Poems 1972–1978* (Winston-Salem, N.C.: Wake Forest University Press, 1979) 11–20. See also Elizabeth Hale Winkler, "Reflections of Derry's Bloody Sunday in Literature," in *Studies in Anglo-Irish Literature,* ed. Heinz Kosok (Bonn: Bouvier Verlag, 1982), 411–21.

8. *The Freedom of the City* (London: Faber and Faber, 1974), 20; further citations made parenthetically in text.

9. Hogan, *O'Casey*, 129.

10. This matter is further explored in Klaus Birker, "The Relationship between the Stage and the Audience in Brian Friel's *The Freedom of the City*," in *The Irish Writer and the City*, ed. Maurice Harmon (Gerrards Cross; Colin Smythe; Totowa, N.J.: Barnes and Noble, 1984), 153–58.

11. For a sense of the issues that fueled this controversy, and of the site's riches, see Breandan O Riordain, "Digging up Dublin," *The Harp* (Spring 1969): 18–22; "Dublin," *Current Archaeology* 2 (September 1970): 312–16; Breandan O Riordain, "Excavations at High Street and Winetavern Street, Dublin," *Medieval Archaeology* 15 (1971): 73–85; Richard Howarth, "What's Wrong at Wood Quay?" *An Taisce* 1, no. 5 (October-December 1977): 4–8.

12. Christopher Murray, Review of *Volunteers, Irish University Review* 10, no. 1 (Spring 1980): 171.

13. *Volunteers* (London: Faber and Faber, 1979), 46; further citations made parenthetically in text.

14. *The Playboy of the Western World*, in *J. M. Synge Collected Works: Plays, Book II*, ed. Ann Saddlemyer (London: Oxford University Press, 1968), 133.

15. Seamus Heaney, review of *Volunteers, Times Literary Supplement*, 21 March 1975; reprinted in Seamus Heaney, *Preoccupations: Selected Prose 1968–1978* (London: Faber and Faber, 1980), 215. *Volunteers* coincides with Heaney's own poetic mining of the Nordic lode; see in particular *North* (London: Faber and Faber, 1975). For some of the connections between Heaney and Friel in this regard, see Ruth Niel, "Digging into History: A Reading of Brian Friel's *Volunteers* and Seamus Heaney's 'Viking Dublin: Trial Pieces,'" *Irish University Review* 16, no. 1 (Spring 1986): 35–47.

16. *Hamlet* 1.5.172.

17. Heaney, *Preoccupations*, 215.

18. Ibid.

19. Murray, *Volunteers*, 171.

20. Deane, *Friel: Plays*, 17.

21. *Living Quarters* (London: Faber and Faber, 1978), 48; further citations made parenthetically in text.

22. This aspect of the play has been singled out as a significant example of independent-mindedness in contemporary Irish theater. See Hogan, *O'Casey*, 58.

23. Ibid., 130.

24. *Aristocrats* (Dublin: Gallery Books, 1980), 39; further citations made parenthetically in text.

25. "Extracts from a Sporadic Diary" in *The Writers: A Sense of Ireland*, ed. Andrew Carpenter and Peter Fallon (New York: George Braziller), 43.

26. Richard Kearney, "Language Play: Brian Friel and Ireland's Verbal Theatre," *Studies* 72 (Spring 1983): 24 (Kearney's emphasis).

27. Declan Kiberd, "Brian Friel's *Faith Healer*" in *Irish Writers and Society at Large*, ed. Masaru Sekine (Gerrards Cross: Colin Smythe, 1985), 106.

28. Hogan, *O'Casey,* 131.

29. *Faith Healer* (London: Faber and Faber, 1980), 13; further citations made parenthetically in text.

30. Deane, *Friel: Plays,* 20.

31. Irving Wardle, the *London Times,* 13 May 1981.

32. Deane, *Friel: Plays,* 22.

33. *Translations* (London: Faber and Faber, 1981), 10; further citations made parenthetically in text.

34. P. J. Dowling, *The Hedge Schools of Ireland* (Cork: The Mercier Press, 1968), 35–36.

35. For a comprehensive treatment of the stereotypical Irishman, see L. P. Curtis, Jr., *Apes and Angels* (Washington, D.C.: Smithsonian Institution Press, 1971), *passim.*

36. J. M. Andrews, *A Paper Landscape* (Oxford: Oxford University Press, 1975) is a history of the Ordnance Survey in Ireland. For a sense of one important contemporary participant in the survey, see R. Barry O'Brien, *Thomas Drummond: Life and Letters* (London: Kegan Paul, Trench, 1889), 21–58. On this dimension of the play see Brian Friel, John Andrews, and Kevin Barry, "Translations and A Paper Landscape: Between Fiction and History," *The Crane Bag* 7, no. 2 (1983): 118–24.

37. In *The Freedom of the City,* Skinner defends his parting act of vandalism, stabbing the portrait of a city father with the mayoral ceremonial sword, with the words, "Allow me my gesture" (89).

38. For an important critique of Friel's depiction of the Ordnance Survey, see the remarks of John Andrews in Friel, Andrews, and Barry, "Translations," 120–22.

39. Ibid., 121.

40. The lines Hugh is trying to remember are from the *Aeneid,* Book I, 1:12–22.

41. 'Extracts from a Sporadic Diary', in *Ireland and the Arts,* ed. Tim Pat Coogan (London: Quartet, n.d.), 60.

42. On the question of examining Friel's plays chronologically, it must be noted at this point that no formal discussion of his sketch, *American Welcome,* staged by the Actors Theater of Louisville during its Festival of New American Plays in March 1980, has been included in this study, though it too reveals Friel's preoccupation with language and cultural coding. The three-page text of this sketch will be found in Stanley Richards, ed., *Best Short Plays 1981* (Radnor, Penn.: Chilton Book Co., 1981), 112–14. Regarding Friel's conception of *Translations* and *The Communication Cord* as a pair, see Kearney, "Language Play," 46.

43. *The Communication Cord* (London: Faber and Faber, 1983), 18; further citations made parenthetically in text.

44. Richard Kearney, "Friel and the Politics of Language Play," *Massachusetts Review* 28, no. 3 (Fall 1987): 513.

45. James Coakley, "Chekhov in Ireland: Brief Notes on Friel's Philadelphia," *Comparative Drama* 7, no. 3 (Fall 1973): 191–97.

46. See Anton Chekhov, *The Three Sisters: An Authoritative Text Edition,*

trans. Tyrone Guthrie and Leonid Kipnis, with critical material selected and introduced by Henry Popkin (New York: Avon Books, 1965).

47. *Living Quarters,* 23.

48. *Three Sisters: A Translation.* (Dublin: Gallery Books, 1981); the remark is quoted on the dust jacket; further citations made parenthetically in text.

49. Gillespie, "Saturday Interview."

50. Tyrone Guthrie, "On a New Translation into English of *The Three Sisters,*" in Chekhov, *The Three Sisters,* 117.

51. *Fathers and Sons* (London: Faber and Faber, 1987), title page; further citations made parenthetically in text.

52. *Three Sisters,* 9.

Chapter Five

1. While *Making History* also deals with language, its emphasis is on the politics of linguistic form rather than on the cultural implications of linguistic usages.

2. Or there is what Friel has called his "accidental quartet," Bell, *The Theatre in Ulster,* 106. The quartet consists of *Philadelphia, Here I Come!, The Loves of Cass McGuire, Lovers,* and *Crystal and Fox.*

3. *Translations,* 39.

4. Fergus Linehan, Hugh Leonard, John B. Keane and Brian Friel, "The Future of Irish Drama," *Irish Times,* 12 February 1970.

5. Denis Johnston, "Brian Friel and Modern Irish Drama," *Hibernia,* 7 March 1975: 22.

6. Linehan, Leonard, Keane, Friel, "Irish Drama."

7. Seamus Heaney, Review of *Translations, Times Literary Supplement,* 24 October 1980, p. 1199; Cathleen ni Houlihan is one of Ireland's symbolic names.

8. Linehan, Leonard, Keane, Friel, "Irish Drama."

9. Deane, *Friel: Plays,* 19.

10. "Plays Peasant and Unpeasant," *Times Literary Supplement,* 17 March 1972, p. 305.

11. Ibid.

12. "The Theatre of Hope and Despair," *Everyman* 1 (1968): 21.

13. "Extracts from a Sporadic Diary," in *Ireland and the Arts,* 61.

14. Richard Ellmann, *Four Dubliners* (New York: George Braziller, 1987), 37.

Selected Bibliography

PRIMARY WORKS

Drama

Published Plays

The Enemy Within. Newark, Del.: Proscenium Press, 1975; Dublin: Gallery Press, 1979.

Philadelphia, Here I Come! London: Faber and Faber; New York: Farrar, Straus and Giroux, 1965.

The Loves of Cass McGuire. New York: Noonday Press, 1966; London: Faber and Faber, 1967.

Lovers. London: Faber and Faber, 1969.

Crystal and Fox. London: Faber and Faber, 1970.

Crystal and Fox and The Mundy Scheme. New York: Farrar, Straus and Giroux, 1970.

The Gentle Island. London: Davis-Poynter, 1973.

The Freedom of the City. London: Faber and Faber, 1974.

Living Quarters. London: Faber and Faber, 1978.

Volunteers. London: Faber and Faber, 1979.

Aristocrats. Dublin: Gallery Press, 1980.

Faith Healer. London: Faber and Faber, 1980.

Translations. London: Faber and Faber, 1981.

Three Sisters by Anton Chekhov. Dublin: Gallery Press, 1981.

American Welcome. In *Best Short Plays 1981,* edited by Stanley Richards, 112–14. Radnor, Pa.: Chilton Book Co., 1981.

The Communication Cord. London: Faber and Faber, 1983.

Selected Plays. London: Faber and Faber, 1984; Washington, D.C.: Catholic University of America Press, 1986.

Fathers and Sons. After Turgenev. London: Faber and Faber, 1987.

Making History. London: Faber and Faber, 1988.

Plays Produced on Radio, Television, and Film

A Sort of Freedom. Produced by BBC Northern Ireland Home Service (radio), 1958.

To This Hard House. Produced by BBC Northern Ireland Home Service (radio), 1958.

A Doubtful Paradise. Produced by Group Theatre, Belfast, 1960; BBC Northern Ireland Home Service (radio), 1962.

The Loves of Cass McGuire. BBC Third Programme (radio), 1961.

The Blind Mice. Produced by Eblana Theatre, Dublin, 1963; BBC Northern Ireland Home Service (radio), 1963; Lyric Theatre, Belfast, 1964.
The Founder Members. Produced by BBC Light Programme (radio), 1964.
The Enemy Within. BBC Third Programme (radio), 1963; BBC-TV, 1965.
Philadelphia, Here I Come!. BBC Third Programme (radio), 1965; film, 1970.
Farewell to Ardstraw (with David Hammond). BBC-TV, 1976.

Fiction

The Saucer of Larks. New York: Doubleday; London: Victor Gollancz, 1962.
The Gold in the Sea. New York: Doubleday; London: Victor Gollancz, 1966.
The Saucer of Larks: Stories of Ireland. London: Arrow Books, 1969.
Selected Stories. Dublin: Gallery Press, 1979.
The Diviner. Dublin: The O'Brien Press; London: Allison and Busby, 1983.
"The Child." *The Bell* 18, no. 4 (July 1952): 232–33.
"Nato at Night." *The New Yorker,* 1 April 1961, 105–9.
"Labors of Love." *The Atlantic Monthly,* April 1963, 130–31.
"Downstairs No Upstairs." *The New Yorker,* 24 August 1963, 82–85.

Nonfiction

"For Export Only." *Comonweal,* 15 February 1957, 509–10.
"The Theatre of Hope and Despair." *Everyman* 1 (1968): 17–22.
"A Challenge to *Acorn*." *Acorn* 14 (Autumn 1970): 4.
"Plays Peasant and Unpeasant." *The Times Literary Supplement,* 17 March 1972, 305–6.
"Self-Portrait." *Aquarius* 3 (1972): 17–22.
Untitled essay. In *Enter Certain Players: Edwards-MacLiammoir and The Gate 1928–1978,* edited by Peter Luke, 21–22. Dublin: Dolmen Press, 1978.
"Extracts from a Sporadic Diary." In *The Writers: A Sense of Ireland,* edited by Andrew Carpenter and Peter Fallon, 39–43. Dublin: O'Brien Press; New York: George Braziller, 1980.
"Extracts from a Sporadic Diary." In *Ireland and the Arts,* edited by Tim Pat Coogan, 56–61. London: Quartet, n.d.
Introduction to Charles McGlinchey, *The Last of the Name.* Belfast: The Blackstaff Press, 1986.

SECONDARY WORKS

Bibliographical and Biographical

Bigsby, C. W. E. *Contemporary Dramatists.* London: St. James Press, 1977.
Carpenter, Charles A. *Modern British Drama.* Golden Tree Bibliographies. Arlington Heights, Ill.: AHM Publishers, 1980.

Hickey, Des and Gus Smith. *A Paler Shade of Green*. London: Leslie Frewin, 1972. U.S. edition, *Flight from the Celtic Twilight*. Indianapolis: Bobbs, Merrill, 1973.

King, Kimball. *Ten Modern Irish Playwrights*. New York: Garland, 1979.

Mikhail, E. H. *A Research Guide to Modern Irish Dramatists*. Troy, N.Y.: Whitston Publishing Co., 1979.

―――. *An Annotated Bibliography of Modern Anglo-Irish Drama*. Troy, N.Y.: Whitston Publishing Co., 1981.

Morison, Graham. "An Ulster Writer: Brian Friel." *Acorn* (Spring 1965): 4–15.

Schlueter, June. "Brian Friel." In *Dictionary of Literary Biography*, ed. Stanley Weintraub, vol. 13, 179–85. Detroit: Gale Research, 1982.

Book-length Studies

Dantanus, Ulf. *Brian Friel: The Growth of an Irish Dramatist*. Gothenburg Studies in English 59. Gothenburg, Sweden: Acta Universitatis Gothoburgensis, 1985; Atlantic Heights, N.J.: Humanities Press, 1986. A survey of Friel's career, particularly informative on the early plays, but rather disorganized and elementary with the later works. The book begins with the argument that Friel's work exemplifies "two dichotomies of place in Irish history," East-West and North-South. This argument is smothered in the welter of detail provided in connection with Friel's stories and unpublished plays, and remains undeveloped throughout. Useful factually, and contains a full bibliography.

―――. *Brian Friel. A Study*. London: Faber and Faber, 1988. Revised and updated version of the above.

Maxwell, D. E. S. *Brian Friel*. Lewisburg, Penn.: Bucknell University Press, 1973. A brief, penetrating, informative account of Friel's career up to and including the production of *The Freedom of the City*. Particularly sensitive to Friel's background and to his use of language.

Articles and Parts of Books

A. W. "Introducing Brian Friel." *Acorn* 14 (November 1970): 25–28.

Allen, Walter. *The Short Story in English*. Oxford: Clarendon Press, 1981. Contains sensitive remarks in passing on Friel's stories.

Andrews, J. M. *A Paper Landscape*. Oxford: Oxford University Press, 1975. Essential for detailed study of the background to *Translations*.

Bell, Sam Hanna. *The Theatre in Ulster*. Dublin: Gill and Macmillan, 1972. A standard work.

Bertha, Csilla. "Tragedies of National Fate: a Comparison between Brian Friel's *Translations* and its Hungarian Counterpart, András Sutö's *A Szuzai menyegaö*." Irish University Review 17, no. 2 (Autumn 1987): pp. 207–22. A valuable, fascinating essay in comparative literature.

Birker, Klaus. "The Relationship between the Stage and the Audience in Brian

Friel's *The Freedom of the City.*" In *The Irish Playwright and the City,* edited by Maurice Harmon, 153–58. Gerrards Cross: Colin Smythe; Totowa, N.J.: Barnes and Noble, 1984. A technical discussion of one aspect of the play's dramaturgical interest.

Boland, Eavan. "The Northern Writers' Crisis of Conscience." A series of three articles in the *Irish Times,* 12, 13, and 14 August 1970. Testimony from a number of Northern writers, including Friel, on their backgrounds and outlooks.

Bordinat, Philip. "Tragedy Through Comedy in Plays by Brendan Behan and Brian Friel." *West Virginia University Papers in Philology* 29 (1983): 84–91. A characterization of "the human comedy" in Friel's "epic," *The Freedom of the City.*

Brown, Terence. *Ireland: A Social and Cultural History 1922–79.* Glasgow: Fontana Paperbacks, 1981. The standard work.

Browne, Joseph. "Violent Prophesies: The Writer and Northern Ireland." *Eire-Ireland,* 10, no. 2 (Summer 1975): 109–19. A useful introduction to the main preoccupation of Irish culture in the 1970s.

Chekhov, Anton. *The Three Sisters: An Authoritative Text Edition.* Translated by Tyrone Guthrie and Leonid Kipnis. Critical material selected and introduced by Henry Popkin. New York: Avon Books, 1965. The text of the production that Friel saw take shape in Minneapolis in 1963.

Coakley, James. "Chekhov in Ireland: Brief Notes on Friel's *Philadelphia.*" *Comparative Drama* 7, no. 3 (Fall 1973): 191–97. Focuses on the play's handling of "that most Chekhovian of rituals: departure or leavetaking."

Connolly, Sean. "Dreaming History: Brian Friel's *Translations,*" *Theatre Ireland* 13 (Autumn 1987): 42–44. An informative negative critique of Friel's use of historical sources in *Translations.*

Curran, Frank. *Derry: Countdown to Disaster.* Dublin: Gill and Macmillan, 1986. Useful for political background.

Deane, Seamus. "The Writer and the Troubles." *Threshold* 25 (Summer 1974): 13–17. The thoughts of Ireland's leading culture critic on the subject.

———. "Brian Friel." In *Celtic Revivals.* London: Faber and Faber, 1986. A summary, with additional analysis, of this critic's thoughts on Friel.

———. Introduction to *Selected Stories,* by Brian Friel. Dublin: Gallery Press, 1979. Essential reading for the cultural context of Friel's stories.

———. "Brian Friel." *Ireland Today,* 978 (1981): 7–10. Informative general introduction.

———. Introduction to *Selected Plays,* by Brian Friel. London: Faber and Faber, 1984. Essential reading for the cultural context and development of Friel's career.

Dowling, P. J. *The Hedge Schools of Ireland.* Cork: Mercier Press, 1968. Useful background for *Translations.*

Farrell, Michael. *Northern Ireland: The Orange State.* London: Pluto Press, 1976. Essential background reading.

Field Day Company, *Ireland's Field Day.* London: Hutchinson, 1985. Republication of the first six of Field Day's continuing series of pamphlets in which, as the preface claims, "the nature of the Irish problem could be explored and, as a result, more successfully confronted than it had been hitherto."

Fitzgibbon, Emelie. "All Change: Contemporary Fashions in the Irish Theater." In *Irish Writers and the Theatre,* edited by Masaru Sekine, 33–46. Gerrards Cross: Colin Smythe; Totowa, N.J.: Barnes and Noble, 1987. p. 33–46. An extremely well-informed survey of the "confusion of styles and modes" in the very recent Irish theatre.

Fitz-Simons, Christopher. *The Irish Theatre.* London: Thames and Hudson, 1983. An overview of Irish theatrical history from its origins to the early 1980s, containing perceptive but necessarily limited remarks on Friel (pp. 193–95).

Forsyth, James. *Tyrone Guthrie.* London: Hamish Hamilton, 1976. Supplement to Guthrie items listed below.

Foster, John Wilson. *Forces and Themes in Ulster Fiction.* Dublin: Gill and Macmillan, 1973. Forceful readings of various Friel stories, including provocative commentary on "Foundry House" and "Ginger Hero." Essential for a sense of the stories' literary context.

Friel, Brian, John Andrews and Kevin Barry, "Translations and A Paper Landscape: Between Fiction and History." *The Crane Bag* 7, no. 2 (1983): 118–24. Essential discussion of *Translations'*s historical background (provided by Andrews) and imaginative foreground (provided by Friel).

Gillespie, Elgy. "The Saturday Interview: Brian Friel." *Irish Times,* 5 September 1981. Contains information on *Three Sisters* and on the fortunes of the Field Day Theatre Company.

Gray, John. "Field Day Five Years On." *Linen Hall Review* 2, no. 2 (Summer 1985): 4–10. Useful supplement to collection of pamphlets cited above.

Grene, Nicholas. "Distancing Drama: Sean O'Casey to Brian Friel." In *Irish Writers and the Theatre,* edited by Masaru Sekine, 47–70. Gerrards Cross: Colin Smythe; Totowa, N.J.: Barnes and Noble, 1987. An examination of four plays—Sean O'Casey's *Plough and the Stars,* Denis Johnston's *Moon in the Yellow River,* Brendan Behan's *Hostage* and Friel's *The Freedom of the City*—"to analyse within them the relationship between theatrical technique and political statement." The plays are seen as "in a sense counter-revolutionary . . . in their profound scepticism about the effect and effectiveness of political liberation."

Guthrie, Tyrone. *A Life in the Theatre.* New York: Limelight Editions, 1985. First published in 1961, this is the autobiography of Friel's theatrical mentor.

————. *In Various Directions: A View of the Theatre.* London: Michael Joseph,

1963. Further stimulating perceptions of the theater by one of the great innovators in the English-speaking theater in the immediate postwar period.

_____. "On a New Translation into English of *The Three Sisters*." In *The Three Sisters: An Authoritative Text Edition*, by Anton Chekhov, translated by Tyrone Guthrie and Leonid Kipnis, critical material selected and introduced by Henry Popkin, 115–17. New York: Avon Books, 1965. An appreciation of Chekhov by Guthrie.

Heaney, Seamus. *Preoccupations: Selected Prose 1968–1978*. London: Faber and Faber, 1980. Reprints review of *Volunteers*.

_____. *North*. London: Faber and Faber, 1975. May be read as an alternative treatment of the concerns of *Volunteers* and *Translations*.

_____. Review of *Translations*. *Times Literary Supplement*, 24 October 1980, p. 1199. An eloquent appreciation of the 1980 Dublin Theatre Festival Production.

_____. Review of *Volunteers*. *Times Literary Supplement*, 21 March 1975, p. 306. An eloquent vindication.

Hogan, Robert. *After the Irish Renaissance*. London: University of Minnesota Press, 1967. A detailed survey, including some useful insights into Friel's early plays.

_____. *"Since O'Casey" and other Essays on Irish Drama*. Gerrards Cross: Colin Smythe; Totowa, N.J.: Barnes and Noble, 1983. An up-to-date supplement to *After the Irish Renaissance*, containing limited commentary on Friel.

Johnston, Denis. "Brian Friel and Modern Irish Drama." *Hibernia*, 7 March 1975, 22. An appraisal of Friel by the then elder statesman of Irish drama.

Kearney, Richard. "Language Play: Brian Friel and Ireland's Verbal Theatre." *Studies* 72, (Spring 1983): 20–56. A sophisticated critique of the verbal dynamics of *Faith Healer*, *Translations* and *The Communication Cord*.

_____. "Friel and the Politics of Language." *Massachusetts Review* 28, no. 3 (Fall 1987): 510–15. An intense, overstated analysis of *The Communication Cord*.

Kiberd, Declan. "Brian Friel's *Faith Healer*." In *Irish Writers and Society at Large*, edited by Masaru Sekine, 106–22. Gerrards Cross: Colin Smythe; Totowa N.J.: Barnes and Noble, 1987. Brilliant and eccentric comparison of *Faith Healer* with J. M. Synge's *Deirdre of the Sorrows* intended to show that "in *Faith Healer* . . . Friel's heroic myth is creatively misinterpreted so that he can redefine heroism for the modern Gaelic world"; by a leading Synge scholar and prominent cultural commentator.

Kilroy, Thomas. "Friel's Plays." Introduction to *The Enemy Within*, by Brian Friel. Dublin: Gallery Press, 1979. A brilliant, brief tribute to Friel's achievement.

Leary, Daniel. "The Romanticism of Brian Friel." In *Contemporary Irish Writing*, edited by James D. Brophy and Raymond J. Porter, 127–42. Boston: Iona College Press/Twayne, 1983. Identifying Friel as "part of the romantic tradition, a sour variety that foresees little for man," the article makes a case for *Faith Healer* being Friel "at his best."

Leonard, Hugh. "Drama: The Turning Point." In *Ireland at the Crossroads,* edited by Patrick Rafroidi and Pierre Joannon, 77–87. Lille: l'Université de Lille, 1978. An interesting view of recent Irish theatre by a leading contributor to it.

Levin, Milton. "Brian Friel: An Introduction." *Eire-Ireland* 7, no. 2 (Summer 1972): 132–36. A review of *Crystal and Fox* and *The Mundy Scheme* in book form ("neither shows the author at his best") together with references to earlier, preferred Friel plays.

Longley, Edna. "Poetry and Politics in Northern Ireland." In *Poetry in the Wars,* 185–211. Newcastle-upon-Tyne: Bloodaxe Books, 1986. The most incisive critique of this problematic subject readily available. Contains challenging views of *Translations,* in particular, and of Field Day as a cultural organization.

McCann, Eamon. *War and an Irish Town.* Harmondsworth: Penguin Books, 1974. Essential background reading.

McMahon, Sean. "The Black North: The Prose Writers of the North of Ireland." *Threshold* 21 (Summer 1967): 158–74. Contains a critique of Friel's stories.

Maxwell, D. E. S. "Imagining the North: Violence and the Writers." *Eire-Ireland* 8, no. 2 (Summer 1973): 91–107. Friel up to and including *The Gentle Island* seen in the context of fellow Northern playwrights Sam Thompson and John Boyd.

————. "Introduction to *The Enemy Within,*" *Journal of Irish Literature* 4, no. 2 (May 1975): 4–6. Background material.

————. *A Critical History of Modern Irish Drama 1891–1980.* Cambridge: Cambridge University Press, 1984. Contains a summary of the author's earlier book on Friel and some rather perfunctory comments on Friel's output since *The Freedom of the City.*

Miner, Edmund J. "Homecoming: The Theme of Disillusionment in Brian Friel's Short Stories." *Kansas Quarterly* 9, no. 2 (Spring 1977): 92–99. A sentimental treatment of "Among the Ruins" and "Foundry House" as stories that "serve to illustrate as well as any Brian Friel's pervasive theme of disillusionment, a subject which characterizes both his short fiction and his drama."

Moody, T. N. and F. X. Martin, eds. *The Course of Irish History* (Cork: Mercier Press, 1967. Scholarly essays by various expert hands on Ireland through the ages.

Murphy, Dervla. *A Place Apart.* London: Penguin, 1980. An invaluable view of contemporary Northern Irish society. For background to Friel see, in particular, chapter 4, "Derry is Different" (73–98).

Murray, Christopher. "Irish Drama in Transition 1966–1978." *Etudes Irlandaises,* Nouvelle Serie 4 (December 1979): 187–308. An important analytical overview, providing a literary context for a commentary on Friel's work.

————. Review of *Translations. Irish University Review* 11, no. 2 (Autumn 1981): 238–39. Makes a brief, insightful case for *Translations* as "surely Friel's masterpiece."

————. Review of *Volunteers. Irish University Review* 10, no. 1 (Spring 1980):

170–71. A brief, appreciative notice, though *Volunteers* is "a long way behind
. . . *Aristocrats*."

――――. "Recent Irish Drama." In Kosok, Heinz (ed.). *Studies in Anglo-Irish Literature*. edited by Heinz Kosok, 439–43. Bonn: Bouvier Verlag Herbert
Grundmann, 1982. Covers plays staged in Ireland between May 1979 and
May 1981, including *Translations,* and concluding that "the Irish theatre is in a
very healthy state." Includes a list of productions in period covered.

Niel, Ruth. "Digging into History: A Reading of Brian Friel's *Volunteers* and
Seamus Heaney's 'Viking Dublin: Trial Pieces'." *Irish University Review* 16,
no. 1 (Spring 1986): 35–47. Commentary on Viking conceits in Friel's play
and Heaney's poem. Useful as one of the few pieces of criticism on what is one
of Friel's very strongest plays.

O'Brien, R. Barry. *Thomas Drummond: Life and Letters*. London: Kegan Paul
Trench, 1889. Contains useful information (pp. 21–58) on one of the important contributors to the Ordnance Survey in Ireland: useful background
for *Translations*.

Liam de. Paor, *Divided Ulster*. Harmondsworth: Penguin Books, 1970. Good
long-range historical overview and analysis of contemporary events.

Rafroidi, Patrick, Raymond Popot, and William Parker. *Aspects of the Irish
Theatre*. Lille: l'Université de Lille, 1972. A comprehensive compilation of
survey-oriented essays in which Friel receives only passing reference.

Robbins, Ronald. "Friel's Modern Fox and Grapes Fable." *Eire-Ireland* 21, no. 4
(Winter 1986): 66–76. "Friel exploits folk material to fashion a dark fable."

Theatre Ireland 2 (January/May 1983): 66–69. A "collective review" of *The
Communication Cord*.

Timm, Eitel F. "Modern Mind, Myth, and History: Brian Friel's *Translations*."
In Kosok, Heinz (ed.). *Studies in Anglo-Irish Literature,* edited by Heinz
Kosok, 447–53. Bonn: Bouvier Verlag Herbert Brundmann, 1982. An "ab-
stract" treatment of the play concerned with the identity crisis of the modern
Irish mind.

Winkler, Elizabeth Hale. "Brian Friel's *The Freedom of the City:* Historical Actuality and Dramatic Imagination." *Canadian Journal of Irish Studies* 7, no. 1:
12–31. An essential source study.

――――. "Eejitin' About: Adolescence in Friel and Keane." *Eire-Ireland* 16, no. 3
(Fall 1981): 128–44. An examination of a Friel character type: "a psychologi-
cally unstable young man who hides his insecurity behind a mask of flippancy"
(an echo of Skinner's epitaphic words in *The Freedom of the City*). Skinner is included, as are Gar O'Donnell (*Philadelphia*), Shane (*The Gentle Island*), and
Ben (*Living Quarters*).

――――. "Reflections of Derry's Bloody Sunday in Literature." In Kosok, Heinz
(ed.). *Studies in Anglo-Irish Literature,* edited by Heinz Kosok, 411–21.
Bonn: Bouvier Verlag Grundmann, 1982. Further source and contextual material for *The Freedom of the City*.

Index